PHILIP'S

FAMILY WORLD ATLAS

Published in Great Britain in 1995
by George Philip Limited,
an imprint of Reed Consumer Books Limited,
Michelin House, 81 Fulham Road, London SW3 6RB
and Auckland, Melbourne, Singapore and Toronto

Cartography by Philip's

Copyright © 1995 Reed International Books Limited

ISBN 0-540-06153-0

A CIP catalogue record for this book is available from
the British Library

Printed in Hong Kong

CONTENTS

iv **World Statistics: Countries**

I **Key to Map Symbols**
  The World: Physical

2–3 **The World: Political** 1:80M

4 **The Arctic and
  Antarctica** 1:50M

5 **Europe: Political** 1:20M

6–7 **Scandinavia and the Baltic
  Lands** 1:5M

8–9 **England and Wales** 1:2M

10 **Scotland** 1:2M

11 **Ireland** 1:2M

12 **France** 1:5M

13 **Spain and Portugal** 1:5M

14–15 **Italy and the Balkan
  States** 1:5M

16–17 **Central Europe** 1:5M

18–19 **Eastern Europe, Russia and
  Central Asia** 1:20M

20 **Asia: Political** 1:50M

21 **Japan** 1:10M
  Southern Japan 1:5M

22 **China** 1:20M

23 **South-east Asia** 1:20M

24 **Southern Asia** 1:20M

25 **South-west Asia** 1:20M

26–27 **Northern Africa** 1:15M

28–29 **Central and Southern
  Africa** 1:15M

30 **Africa: Political** 1:40M

31 **New Zealand** 1:6M
  **New Zealand and
  S.W. Pacific** 1:60M
  **Fiji, Tonga and Samoan
  Islands** 1:12M

32–33 **Australia** 1:12M

34–35 **Canada** 1:15M
  Alaska 1:30M

36–37 **United States** 1:12M
  Hawaii 1:10M

38–39 **Mexico, Central America
  and the West Indies** 1:15M
  **Leeward Islands,
  Windward Islands,
  Trinidad and Tobago,
  and Jamaica** 1:5M
  Panama Canal 1:1M

40–41 **South America – North** 1:16M

42 **South America – South** 1:16M

43–48 **Index**

WORLD STATISTICS: COUNTRIES

This alphabetical list includes all the countries and territories of the world. If a territory is not completely independent, then the country it is associated with is named. The area figures give the total area of land, inland water and ice. Units for areas and populations are thousands. The figures are the latest available, usually 1993.

Country/ Territory	Area km² Thousands	Population Thousands	Capital
Afghanistan	652	19,062	Kabul
Albania	28.8	3,363	Tirana
Algeria	2,382	26,346	Algiers
American Samoa (US)	0.20	50	Pago Pago
Andorra	0.45	58	Andorra la Vella
Angola	1,247	10,609	Luanda
Anguilla (UK)	0.09	9	The Valley
Antigua & Barbuda	0.44	66	St John's
Argentina	2,767	33,101	Buenos Aires
Armenia	29.8	3,677	Yerevan
Aruba (Neths)	0.19	62	Oranjestad
Australia	7,687	17,529	Canberra
Austria	83.9	7,884	Vienna
Azerbaijan	86.6	7,398	Baku
Azores (Port)	2.2	260	Ponta Delgada
Bahamas	13.9	262	Nassau
Bahrain	0.68	533	Manama
Bangladesh	144	119,288	Dhaka
Barbados	0.43	259	Bridgetown
Belarus	207.6	10,297	Minsk
Belau	0.46	16	Koror
Belgium	30.5	9,998	Brussels
Belize	23	198	Belmopan
Benin	113	4,889	Porto-Novo
Bermuda (UK)	0.05	62	Hamilton
Bhutan	47	1,612	Thimphu
Bolivia	1,099	7,832	La Paz/Sucre
Bosnia-Herzegovina	51.2	4,366	Sarajevo
Botswana	582	1,373	Gaborone
Brazil	8,512	156,275	Brasília
Brunei	5.8	270	Bandar Seri Begawan
Bulgaria	111	8,963	Sofia
Burkina Faso	274	9,490	Ouagadougou
Burma (Myanmar)	677	43,668	Rangoon
Burundi	27.8	5,786	Bujumbura
Cambodia	181	9,054	Phnom Penh
Cameroon	475	12,198	Yaoundé
Canada	9,976	27,562	Ottawa
Canary Is. (Spain)	7.3	1,700	Las Palmas/ Santa Cruz
Cape Verde Is.	4	384	Praia
Cayman Is. (UK)	0.26	29	George Town
Central African Rep.	623	3,173	Bangui
Chad	1,284	5,961	Ndjamena
Chile	757	13,599	Santiago
China	9,597	1,187,997	Beijing (Peking)
Colombia	1,139	33,424	Bogotá
Comoros	2.2	585	Moroni
Congo	342	2,368	Brazzaville
Cook Is. (NZ)	0.24	17	Avarua
Costa Rica	51.1	3,099	San José
Croatia	56.5	4,764	Zagreb
Cuba	111	10,822	Havana
Cyprus	9.3	716	Nicosia
Czech Republic	78.9	10,299	Prague
Denmark	43.1	5,170	Copenhagen
Djibouti	23.2	467	Djibouti
Dominica	0.75	72	Roseau
Dominican Republic	48.7	7,471	Santo Domingo
Ecuador	284	10,741	Quito
Egypt	1,001	55,163	Cairo
El Salvador	21	5,396	San Salvador
Equatorial Guinea	28.1	369	Malabo
Eritrea	94	3,500	Asmera
Estonia	44.7	1,542	Tallinn
Ethiopia	1,128	55,117	Addis Ababa
Falkland Is. (UK)	12.2	2	Stanley
Faroe Is. (Den.)	1.4	47	Tórshavn
Fiji	18.3	739	Suva
Finland	338	5,042	Helsinki
France	552	57,372	Paris
French Guiana (Fr.)	90	104	Cayenne
French Polynesia (Fr.)	4	207	Papeete
Gabon	268	1,237	Libreville
Gambia, The	11.3	878	Banjul
Georgia	69.7	5,471	Tbilisi
Germany	357	80,569	Berlin/Bonn

Country/ Territory	Area km² Thousands	Population Thousands	Capital
Ghana	239	15,400	Accra
Gibraltar (UK)	0.007	31	Gibraltar Town
Greece	132	10,300	Athens
Greenland (Den.)	2,176	57	Godthåb (Nuuk)
Grenada	0.34	91	St George's
Guadeloupe (Fr.)	1.7	400	Basse-Terre
Guam (US)	0.55	139	Agana
Guatemala	109	9,745	Guatemala City
Guinea	246	6,116	Conakry
Guinea-Bissau	36.1	1,006	Bissau
Guyana	215	808	Georgetown
Haiti	27.8	6,764	Port-au-Prince
Honduras	112	5,462	Tegucigalpa
Hong Kong (UK)	1.1	5,801	Victoria
Hungary	93	10,313	Budapest
Iceland	103	260	Reykjavik
India	3,288	879,548	New Delhi
Indonesia	1,905	191,170	Jakarta
Iran	1,648	56,964	Tehran
Iraq	438	19,290	Baghdad
Ireland	70.3	3,547	Dublin
Israel	27	4,946	Jerusalem
Italy	301	57,782	Rome
Ivory Coast	322	12,910	Abidjan/ Yamoussoukro
Jamaica	11	2,469	Kingston
Japan	378	124,336	Tokyo
Jordan	89.2	4,291	Amman
Kazakhstan	2,717	17,038	Alma Ata
Kenya	580	26,985	Nairobi
Kiribati	0.72	74	Tarawa
Korea, North	121	22,618	Pyongyang
Korea, South	99	43,663	Seoul
Kuwait	17.8	1,970	Kuwait City
Kyrgyzstan	198.5	4,472	Bishkek
Laos	237	4,469	Vientiane
Latvia	65	2,632	Riga
Lebanon	10.4	2,838	Beirut
Lesotho	30.4	1,836	Maseru
Liberia	111	2,580	Monrovia
Libya	1,760	4,875	Tripoli
Liechtenstein	0.16	28	Vaduz
Lithuania	65.2	3,759	Vilnius
Luxembourg	2.6	390	Luxembourg
Macau (Port.)	0.02	374	Macau
Macedonia	25.3	2,174	Skopje
Madagascar	587	12,827	Antananarivo
Madeira (Port.)	0.81	280	Funchal
Malawi	118	8,823	Lilongwe
Malaysia	330	18,181	Kuala Lumpur
Maldives	0.30	231	Malé
Mali	1,240	9,818	Bamako
Malta	0.32	359	Valletta
Marshall Is.	0.18	49	Dalap-Uliga- Darrit
Martinique (Fr.)	1.1	368	Fort-de-France
Mauritania	1,025	2,143	Nouakchott
Mauritius	2.0	1,084	Port Louis
Mayotte (Fr.)	0.37	84	Mamoundzou
Mexico	1,958	89,538	Mexico City
Micronesia, Fed. States	0.70	110	Palikir
Moldova	33.7	4,458	Kishinev
Monaco	0.002	30	Monaco
Mongolia	1,567	2,310	Ulan Bator
Montserrat (UK)	0.10	11	Plymouth
Morocco	447	26,318	Rabat
Mozambique	802	14,872	Maputo
Namibia	825	1,562	Windhoek
Nauru	0.02	10	Yaren
Nepal	141	20,577	Katmandu
Netherlands	41.5	15,178	Amsterdam
Neths Antilles (Neths)	0.99	175	Willemstad
New Caledonia (Fr.)	19	173	Nouméa
New Zealand	269	3,414	Wellington
Nicaragua	130	4,130	Managua
Niger	1,267	8,252	Niamey
Nigeria	924	88,515	Lagos/Abuja
Northern Mariana Is. (US)	0.48	22	Saipan

Country/ Territory	Area km² Thousands	Population Thousands	Capital
Norway	324	4,286	Oslo
Oman	212	1,637	Muscat
Pakistan	796	115,520	Islamabad
Panama	77.1	2,515	Panama City
Papua New Guinea	463	4,056	Port Moresby
Paraguay	407	4,519	Asunción
Peru	1,285	22,454	Lima
Philippines	300	64,259	Manila
Poland	313	38,356	Warsaw
Portugal	92.4	9,846	Lisbon
Puerto Rico (US)	9	3,580	San Juan
Qatar	11	453	Doha
Réunion (Fr.)	2.5	624	St-Denis
Romania	238	23,185	Bucharest
Russia	17,075	149,527	Moscow
Rwanda	26.3	7,526	Kigali
St Christopher & Nevis	0.36	42	Basseterre
St Lucia	0.62	137	Castries
St Pierre & Miquelon (Fr.)	0.24	6	St Pierre
St Vincent & Grenadines	0.39	109	Kingstown
San Marino	0.06	23	San Marino
São Tomé & Príncipe	0.96	124	São Tomé
Saudi Arabia	2,150	15,922	Riyadh
Senegal	197	7,736	Dakar
Seychelles	0.46	72	Victoria
Sierra Leone	71.7	4,376	Freetown
Singapore	0.62	2,812	Singapore
Slovak Republic	49	5,297	Bratislava
Slovenia	20.3	1,996	Ljubljana
Solomon Is.	28.9	342	Honiara
Somalia	638	9,204	Mogadishu
South Africa	1,220	39,790	Pretoria/ Cape Town
Spain	505	39,085	Madrid
Sri Lanka	65.6	17,405	Colombo
Sudan	2,506	26,656	Khartoum
Surinam	163	438	Paramaribo
Swaziland	17.4	792	Mbabane
Sweden	450	8,678	Stockholm
Switzerland	41.3	6,905	Bern
Syria	185	12,958	Damascus
Taiwan	36	20,659	Taipei
Tajikistan	143.1	5,465	Dushanbe
Tanzania	945	27,829	Dar es Salaam/ Dodoma
Thailand	513	57,760	Bangkok
Togo	56.8	3,763	Lomé
Tonga	0.75	97	Nuku'alofa
Trinidad & Tobago	5.1	1,265	Port of Spain
Tunisia	164	8,410	Tunis
Turkey	779	58,775	Ankara
Turkmenistan	488.1	3,714	Ashkhabad
Turks & Caicos Is. (UK)	0.43	13	Grand Turk
Tuvalu	0.03	12	Funafuti
Uganda	236	18,674	Kampala
Ukraine	603.7	52,200	Kiev
United Arab Emirates	83.6	1,629	Abu Dhabi
United Kingdom	243.3	57,848	London
United States	9,373	255,020	Washington, DC
Uruguay	177	3,131	Montevideo
Uzbekistan	447.4	21,627	Tashkent
Vanuatu	12.2	157	Port Vila
Venezuela	912	20,249	Caracas
Vietnam	332	69,306	Hanoi
Virgin Is. (UK)	0.15	17	Road Town
Virgin Is. (US)	0.34	107	Charlotte Amalie
Wallis & Futuna Is. (Fr.)	0.20	14	Mata-Utu
Western Sahara	266	250	El Aaiún
Western Samoa	2.8	161	Apia
Yemen	528	11,282	Sana
Yugoslavia	102.3	10,469	Belgrade
Zaïre	2,345	39,882	Kinshasa
Zambia	753	8,638	Lusaka
Zimbabwe	391	10,583	Harare

GENERAL REFERENCE

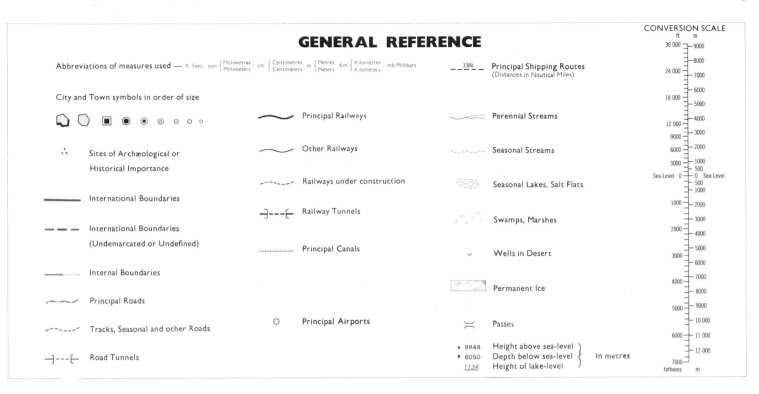

Abbreviations of measures used — ft Feet; mm {Millimetres / Millimeters} cm {Centimetres / Centimeters} m {Metres / Meters} Km {Kilometres / Kilometers} mb Millibars

City and Town symbols in order of size

Sites of Archæological or Historical Importance

International Boundaries

International Boundaries (Undemarcated or Undefined)

Internal Boundaries

Principal Roads

Tracks, Seasonal and other Roads

Road Tunnels

Principal Railways

Other Railways

Railways under construction

Railway Tunnels

Principal Canals

Principal Airports

Principal Shipping Routes (Distances in Nautical Miles)

Perennial Streams

Seasonal Streams

Seasonal Lakes, Salt Flats

Swamps, Marshes

Wells in Desert

Permanent Ice

Passes

▲ 8848 Height above sea-level }
▼ 8050 Depth below sea-level } In metres
_1134_ Height of lake-level }

CONVERSION SCALE

THE WORLD
Physical
1:150 000 000

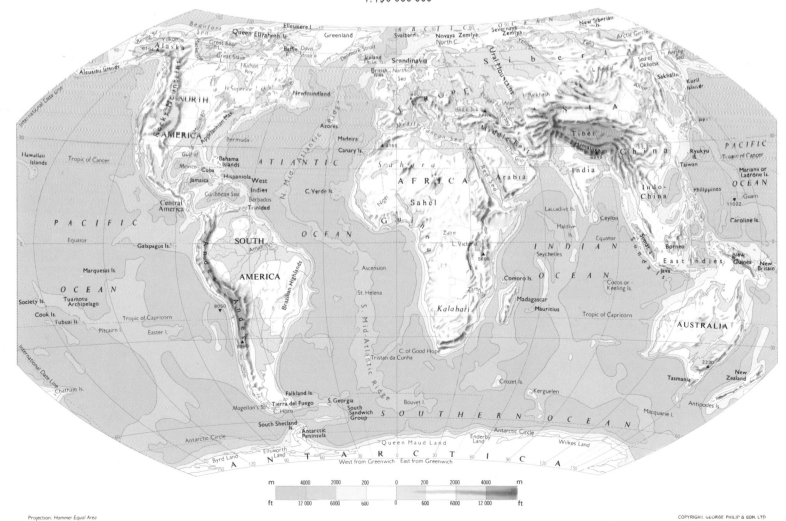

Projection: Hammer Equal Area

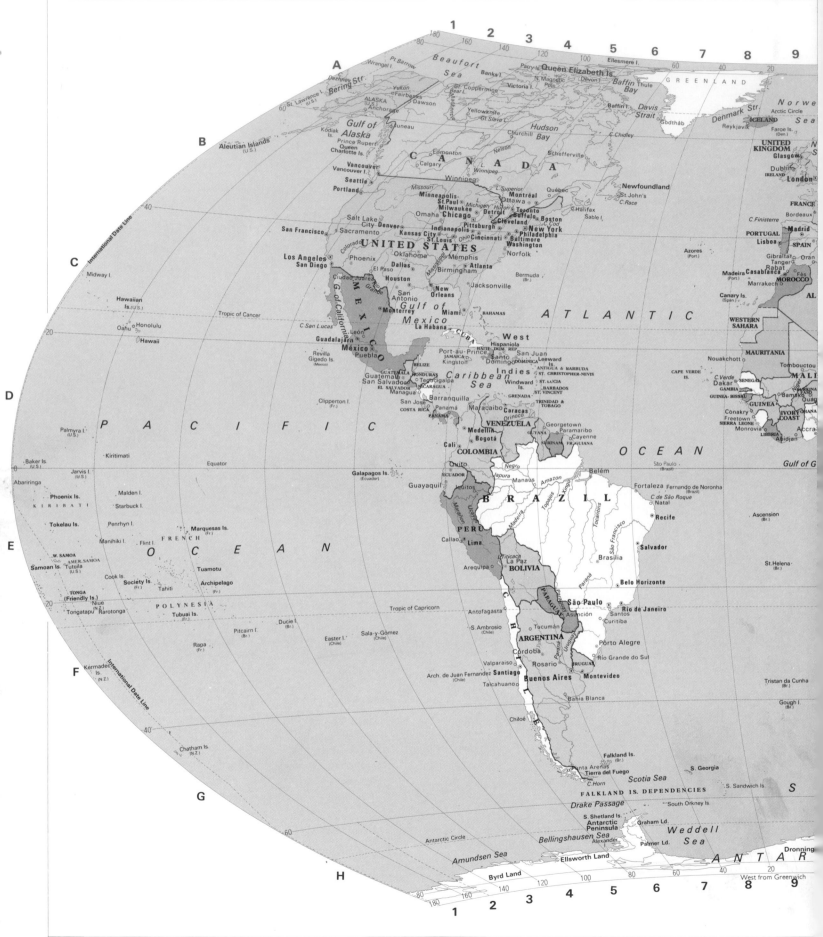

Projection: Hammer Equal Area

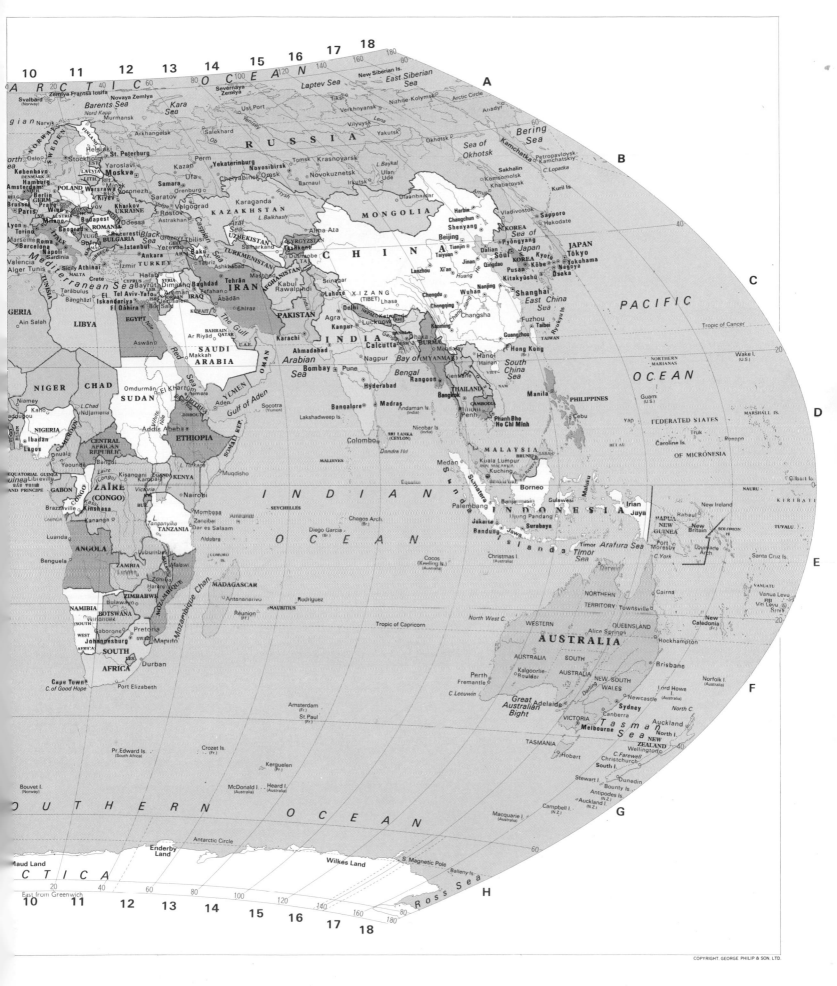

1 : 50 000 000

200   0   200   400   600   800   1000 miles
200   0   400   800   1200   1600 km

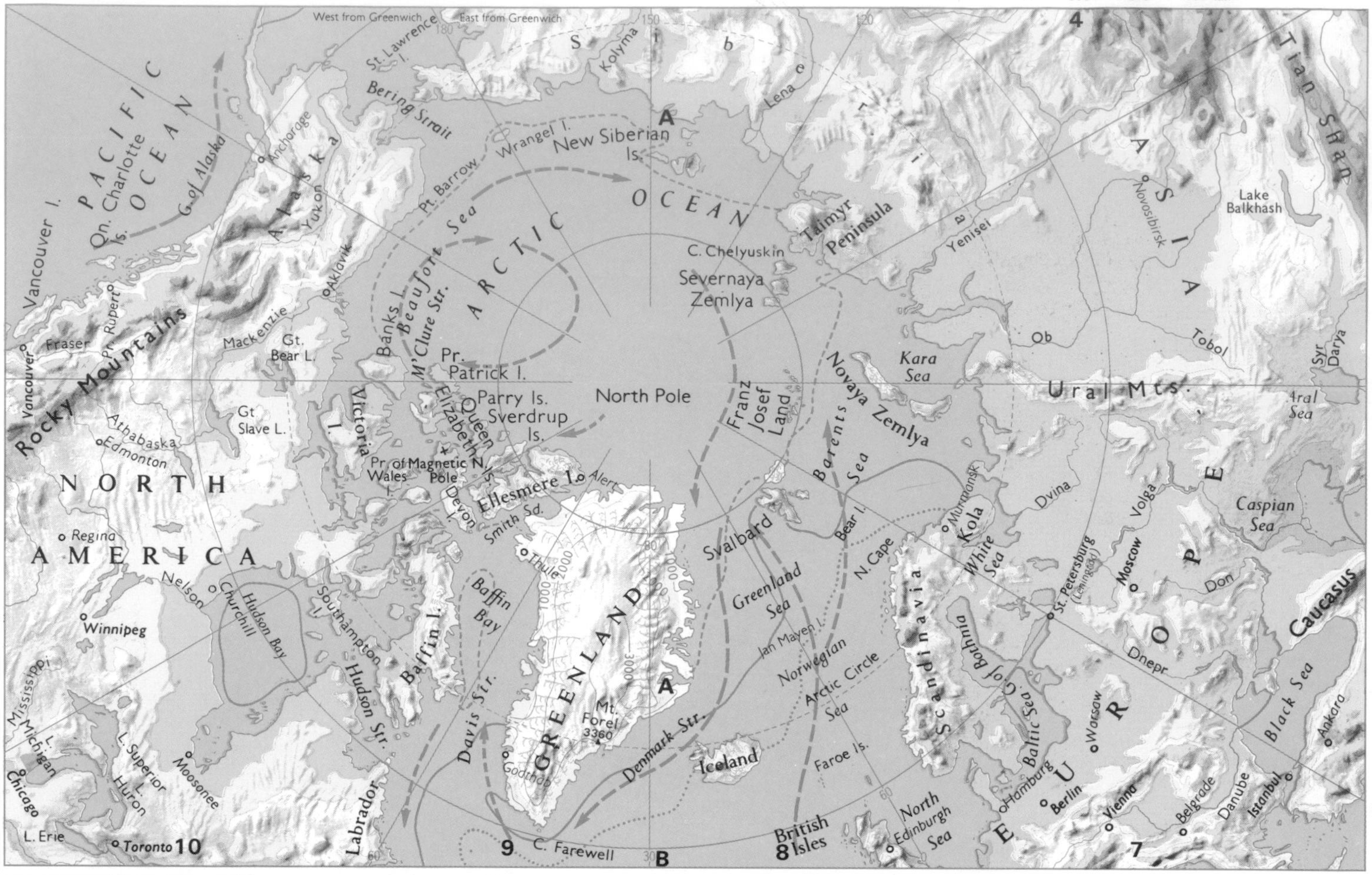

Top map (The Arctic):

West from Greenwich   East from Greenwich

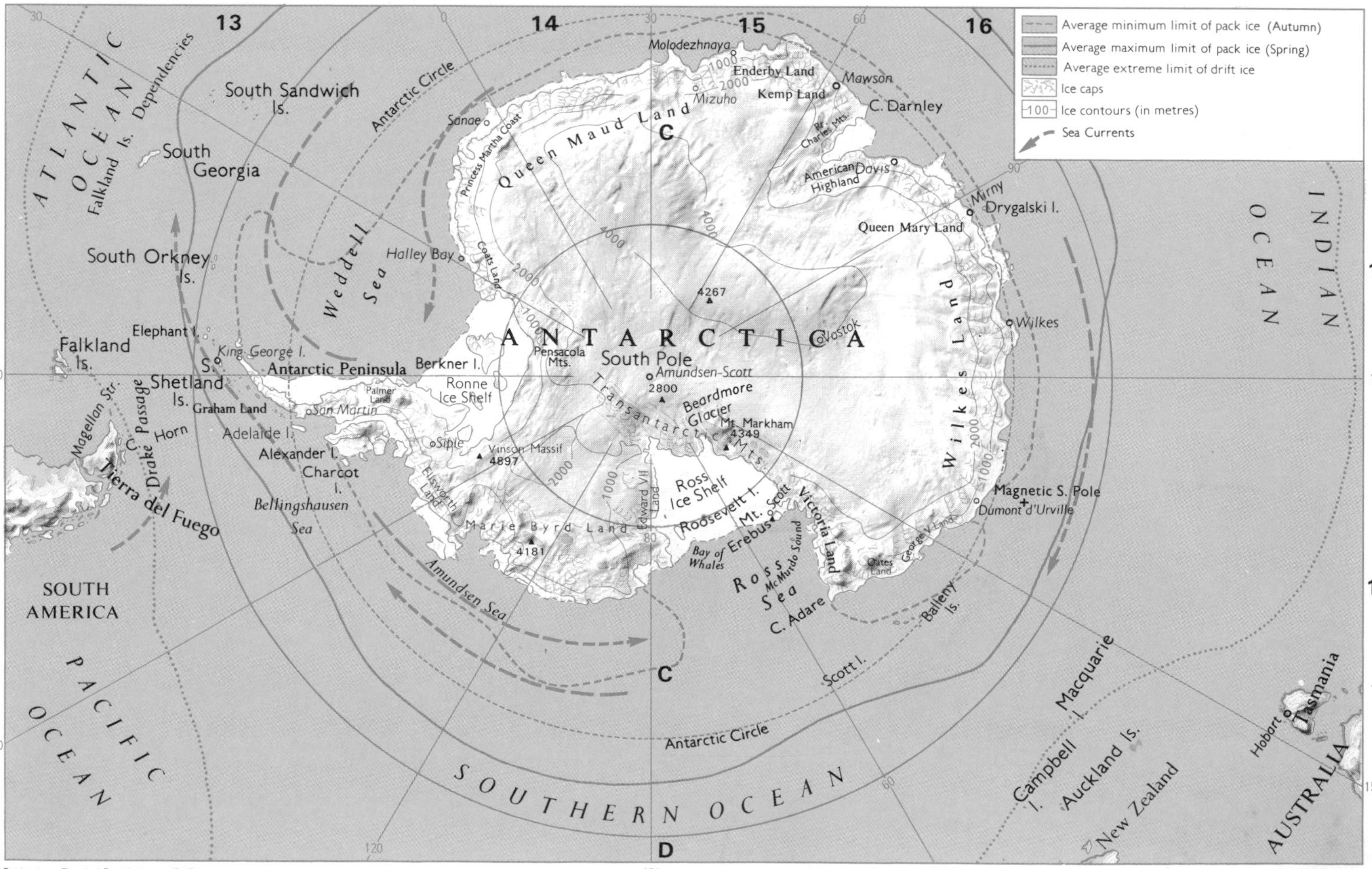

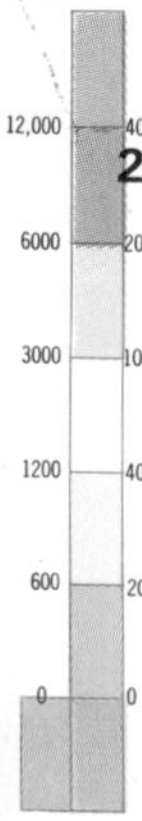

PACIFIC OCEAN

Vancouver I.
Qn. Charlotte Is.
G. of Alaska
Anchorage
Aklavik
Yukon
Alaska
Pt. Barrow
Bering Strait
St. Lawrence I.
Kolyma
Wrangel I.
New Siberian Is.
A
S   I   A   b
Lena
Taimyr Peninsula
C. Chelyuskin
Severnaya Zemlya
ARCTIC OCEAN
Yenisei
Novosibirsk
Lake Balkhash
Tian Shan

Vancouver
Fraser
Rocky Mountains
Athabaska
Edmonton
Gt. Bear L.
Gt. Slave L.
Banks I.
Victoria I.
Beaufort Sea
M'Clure Str.
Pr. Patrick I.
Parry Is.
Queen Elizabeth Is.
Sverdrup Is.
North Pole
Franz Josef Land
Novaya Zemlya
Kara Sea
Barents Sea
Ob
Tobol
Ural Mts.
Aral Sea
Syr Darya

NORTH AMERICA
Regina
Pr. of Wales I.
Magnetic N. Pole
Ellesmere I.
Devon I.
Alert
Smith Sd.
Svalbard
Bear I.
Greenland Sea
Kola
White Sea
St. Petersburg (Leningrad)
Moscow
Caspian Sea
Volga
Don
E U R O P E
Caucasus

Nelson
Winnipeg
Churchill
Hudson Bay
Southampton I.
Baffin I.
Baffin Bay
Thule
GREENLAND
Mt. Forel 3360
A
Jan Mayen I.
Norwegian Sea
Arctic Circle
Scandinavia
G. of Bothnia
Dvina
Dnepr
Black Sea
Ankara

Mississippi
L. Michigan
Chicago
L. Superior
L. Huron
Moosonee
Hudson Str.
Davis Str.
Godthåb
Denmark Str.
Iceland
Faroe Is.
Baltic Sea
Hamburg
Berlin
Warsaw
Vienna
Belgrade
Danube
Istanbul

L. Erie
Toronto
Labrador
C. Farewell
B
North Sea
Edinburgh
British Isles
E

Bottom map (Antarctica):

ATLANTIC OCEAN
Falkland Is. Dependencies
South Sandwich Is.
South Georgia
Antarctic Circle
Molodezhnaya
Enderby Land
Mizuho
Kemp Land
Mawson
C. Darnley
Queen Maud Land
Sanae
Princess Martha Coast
C
Charles Mts.
American Davis Highland
Marny
Drygalski I.

South Orkney Is.
Weddell Sea
Halley Bay
Coats Land
2000
4267
Vostok
Queen Mary Land
Wilkes
INDIAN OCEAN

Falkland Is.
Elephant I.
King George I.
S. Shetland Is.
Graham Land
San Martin
Antarctic Peninsula
Berkner I.
Pensacola Mts.
Ronne Ice Shelf
Palmer Land
South Pole
Amundsen-Scott
ANTARCTICA
2800
Beardmore Glacier
Mt. Markham 4349
Transantarctic Mts.
Wilkes Land
Magnetic S. Pole
Dumont d'Urville

Magellan Str.
Drake Passage
C. Horn
Tierra del Fuego
Adelaide I.
Alexander I.
Charcot I.
Siple
Vinson Massif 4897
Ellsworth Land
Edward VII
Ross Ice Shelf
Roosevelt I.
Mt. Scott
Victoria Land
Scott

PACIFIC OCEAN
Bellingshausen Sea
Marie Byrd Land
4181
Bay of Whales
Mt. Erebus
Ross Sea
McMurdo Sound
C. Adare
Oates Land
Balleny Is.
Macquarie I.

SOUTH AMERICA
Amundsen Sea
C
Scott I.
Antarctic Circle
Campbell I.
Auckland Is.
New Zealand
Tasmania
Hobart
AUSTRALIA

SOUTHERN OCEAN
D
West from Greenwich   180   East from Greenwich

Elevation scale:

ft   m
12,000   4000
6000   2000
3000   1000
1200   400
600   200
0   0

Legend:

— — — Average minimum limit of pack ice (Autumn)
———— Average maximum limit of pack ice (Spring)
·········· Average extreme limit of drift ice
         Ice caps
—100— Ice contours (in metres)
→ Sea Currents

Projection: *Zenithal Equidistant*

The Antarctic Treaty was signed in Washington in 1959 so that scientific and technical research could continue unhampered by international politics. All territorial claims covering land areas south of latitude 60°S have been suspended.

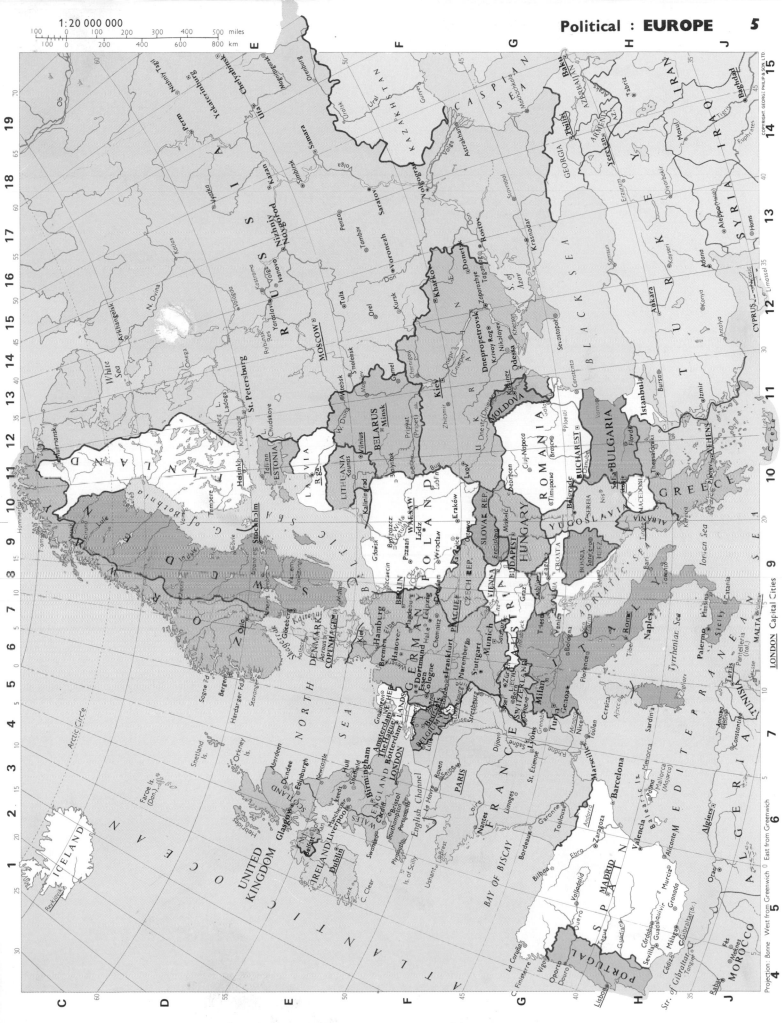

1:20 000 000

LONDON Capital Cities

Projection: Bonne   West from Greenwich 0 East from Greenwich

COPYRIGHT GEORGE PHILIP & SON, LTD

ICELAND
on the same scale
as general map

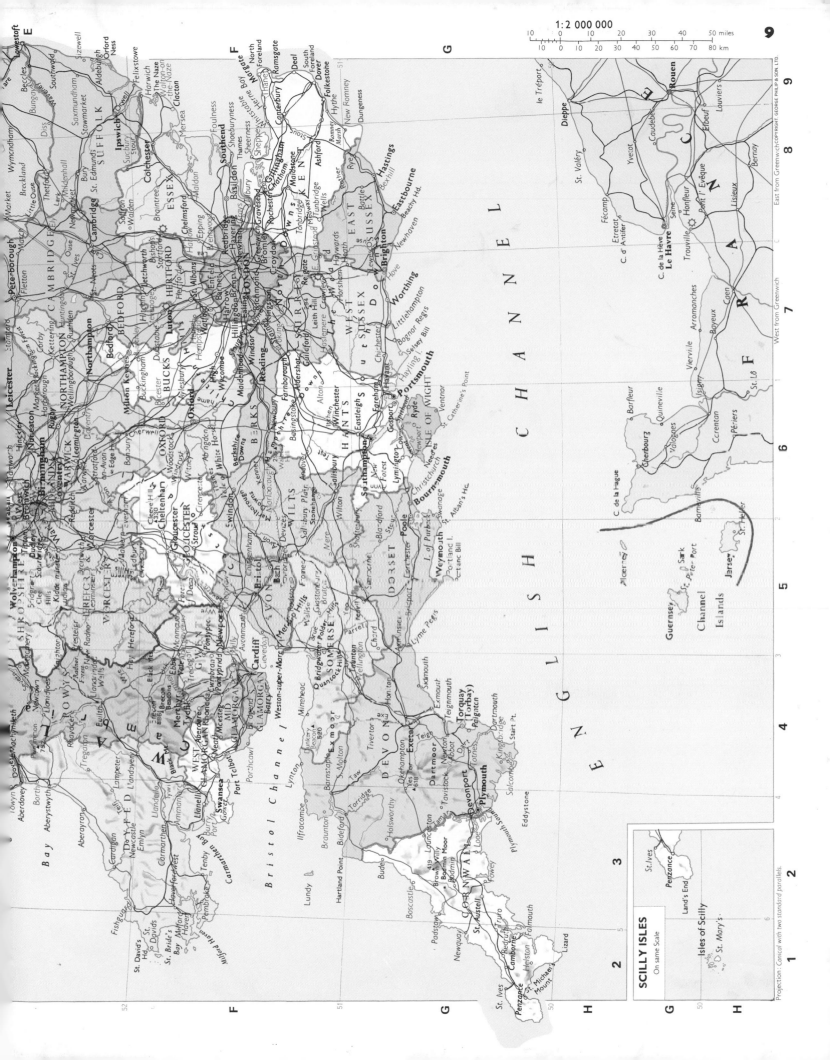

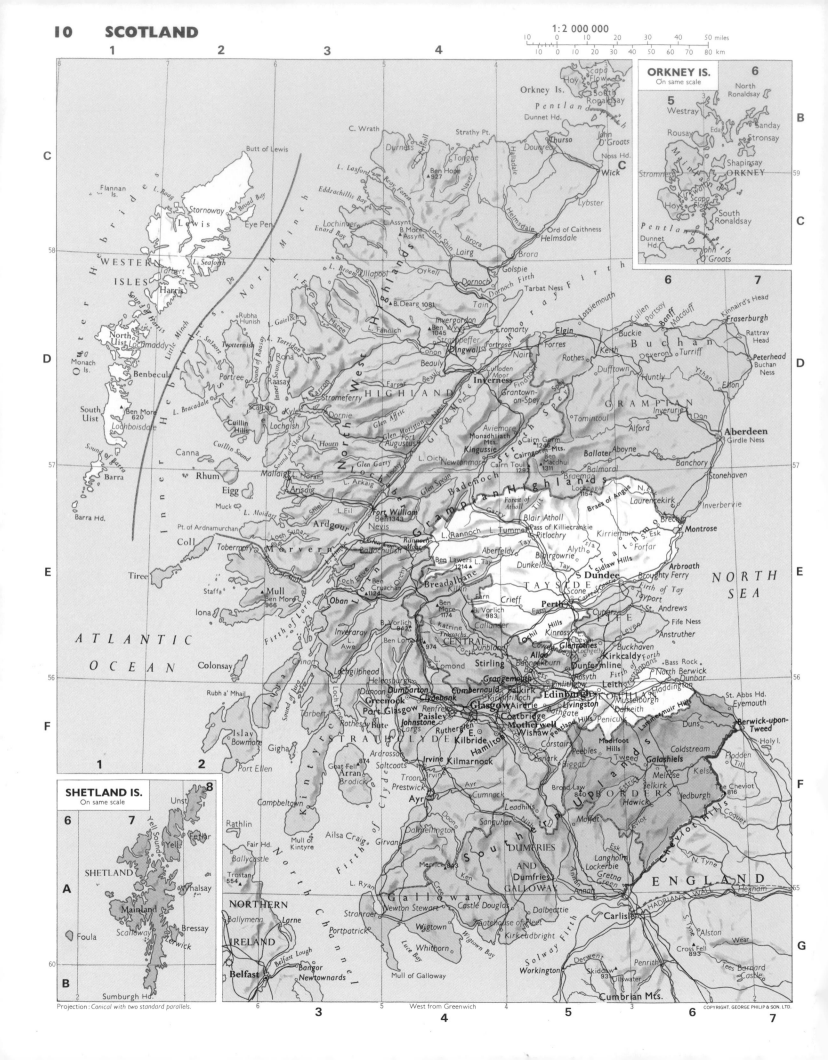

1 : 2 000 000

ORKNEY IS.
On same scale

SHETLAND IS.
On same scale

ATLANTIC OCEAN

NORTH SEA

ENGLAND

NORTHERN IRELAND

Projection : Conical with two standard parallels.

West from Greenwich

COPYRIGHT. GEORGE PHILIP & SON, LTD.

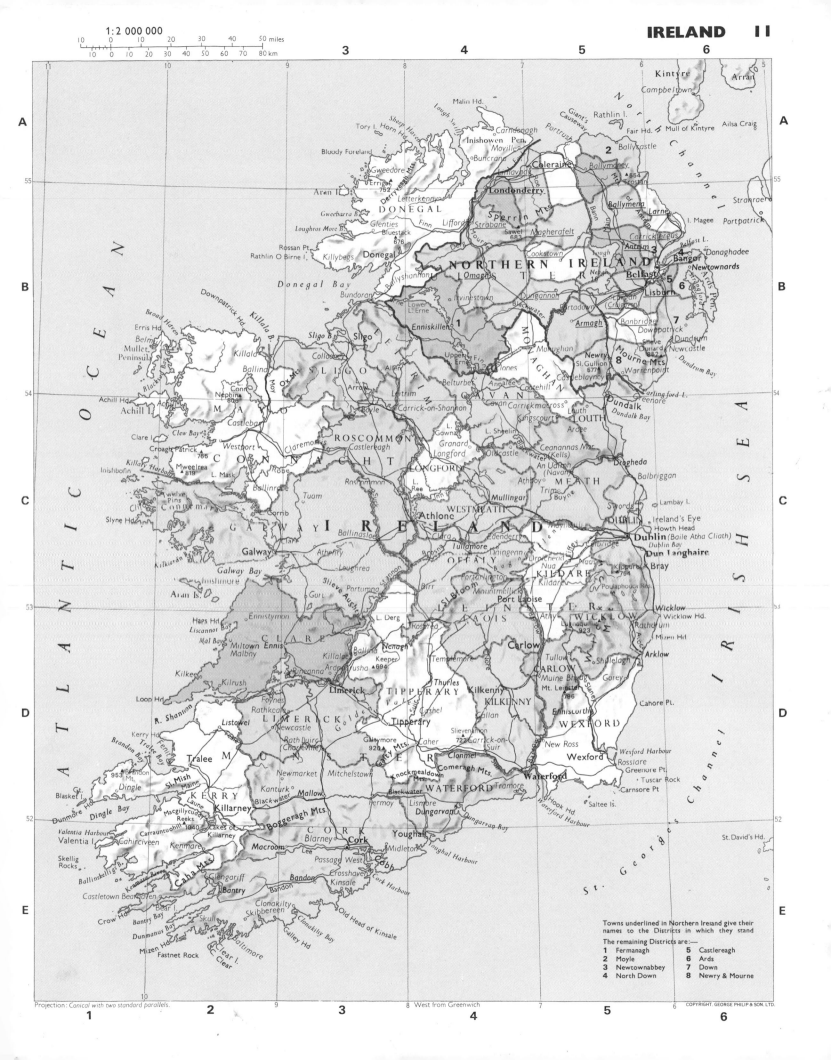

1:2 000 000

Scale: 10 0 10 20 30 40 50 miles
10 0 10 20 30 40 50 60 70 80 km

Towns underlined in Northern Ireland give their
names to the Districts in which they stand

The remaining Districts are:—

1	Fermanagh	5	Castlereagh
2	Moyle	6	Ards
3	Newtownabbey	7	Down
4	North Down	8	Newry & Mourne

Projection: Conical with two standard parallels.

West from Greenwich

COPYRIGHT. GEORGE PHILIP & SON. LTD.

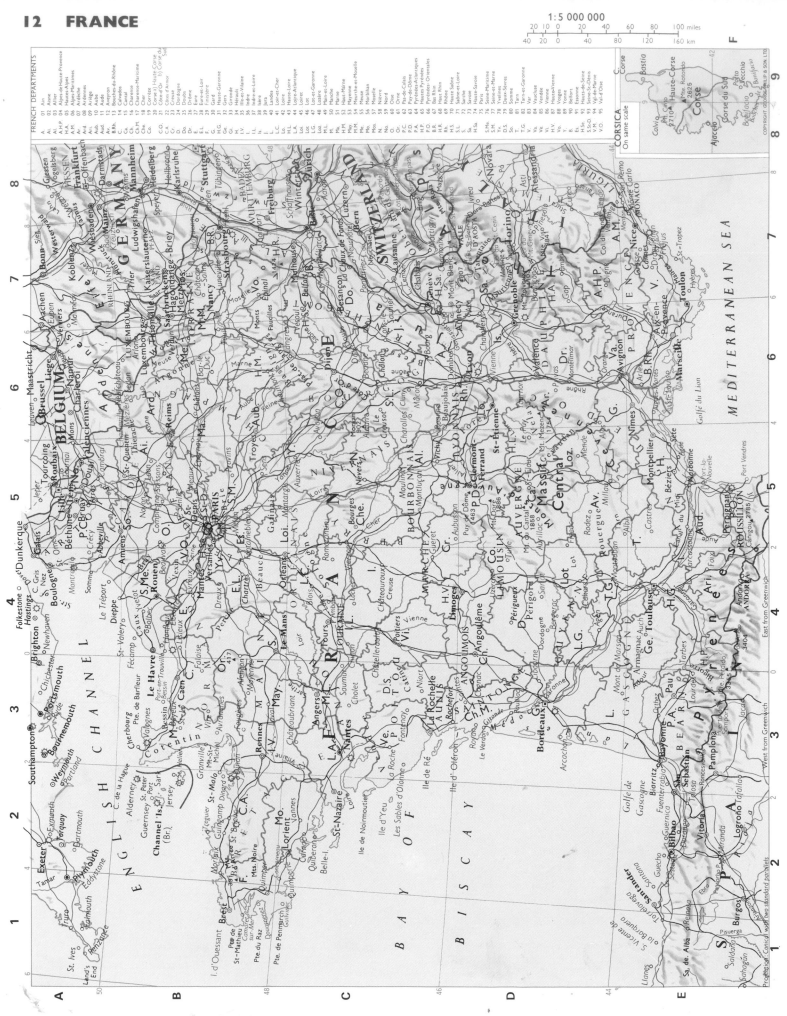

1:5 000 000

FRENCH DEPARTMENTS

A.	01	Ain
Ai.	02	Aisne
Al.	03	Allier
A.H.P.	04	Alpes-de-Haute-Provence
H.A.	05	Hautes-Alpes
A.M.	06	Alpes-Maritimes
Ar.	07	Ardèche
Ard.	08	Ardennes
Ari.	09	Ariège
Au.	10	Aube
Aud.	11	Aude
Av.	12	Aveyron
B.Rh.	13	Bouches-du-Rhône
C.	14	Calvados
Ca.	15	Cantal
Ch.	16	Charente
Ch.M.	17	Charente-Maritime
Che.	18	Cher
Co.	19	Corrèze
	20	a) Corse (Haute-Corse b) Corse du Sud
C.O.	21	Côte-d'Or
C.A.	22	Côtes-d'Armor
Cr.	23	Creuse
D.	24	Dordogne
Do.	25	Doubs
Dr.	26	Drôme
E.	27	Eure
E.L.	28	Eure-et-Loir
F.	29	Finistère
G.	30	Gard
H.G.	31	Haute-Garonne
Ge.	32	Gers
Gi.	33	Gironde
H.	34	Hérault
I.V.	35	Ille-et-Vilaine
I.	36	Indre
I.L.	37	Indre-et-Loire
Is.	38	Isère
J.	39	Jura
L.	40	Landes
L.C.	41	Loir-et-Cher
Loi.	42	Loire
H.L.	43	Haute-Loire
L.A.	44	Loire-Atlantique
Loe.	45	Loiret
Lot	46	Lot
L.G.	47	Lot-et-Garonne
Loz.	48	Lozère
M.L.	49	Maine-et-Loire
Ma.	50	Manche
M.	51	Marne
H.M.	52	Haute-Marne
May.	53	Mayenne
M.M.	54	Meurthe-et-Moselle
Me.	55	Meuse
Mo.	56	Morbihan
Mos.	57	Moselle
N.	58	Nièvre
No.	59	Nord
O.	60	Oise
Or.	61	Orne
P.C.	62	Pas-de-Calais
P.D.	63	Puy-de-Dôme
P.A.	64	Pyrénées-Atlantiques
H.P.	65	Hautes-Pyrénées
P.O.	66	Pyrénées-Orientales
B.R.	67	Bas-Rhin
H.R.	68	Haut-Rhin
Rh.	69	Rhône
H.S.	70	Haute-Saône
S.L.	71	Saône-et-Loire
Sa.	72	Sarthe
Sav.	73	Savoie
H.Sa.	74	Haute-Savoie
	75	Paris
S.Me.	76	Seine-Maritime
S.M.	77	Seine-et-Marne
Y.	78	Yvelines
D.S.	79	Deux-Sèvres
S.	80	Somme
T.	81	Tarn
T.G.	82	Tarn-et-Garonne
Va.	83	Var
Vu.	84	Vaucluse
Ve.	85	Vendée
Vi.	86	Vienne
H.V.	87	Haute-Vienne
Vo.	88	Vosges
B.	89	Yonne
Es.	90	Belfort
	91	Essonne
H.Se.	92	Hauts-de-Seine
S.S.D.	93	Seine-St-Denis
V.M.	94	Val-de-Marne
V.O.	95	Val-d'Oise

CORSICA
On same scale

MEDITERRANEAN SEA

BAY OF BISCAY

ENGLISH CHANNEL

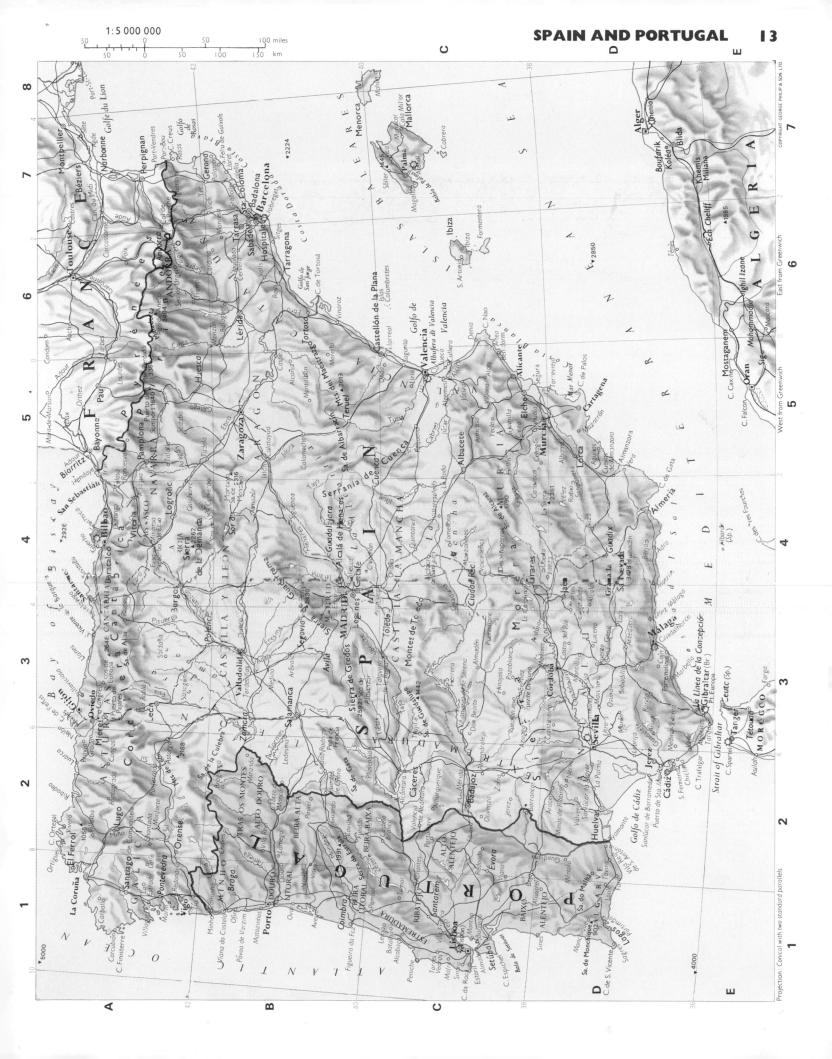

1:5 000 000

Projection: Conical with two standard parallels

COPYRIGHT GEORGE PHILIP & SON, LTD.

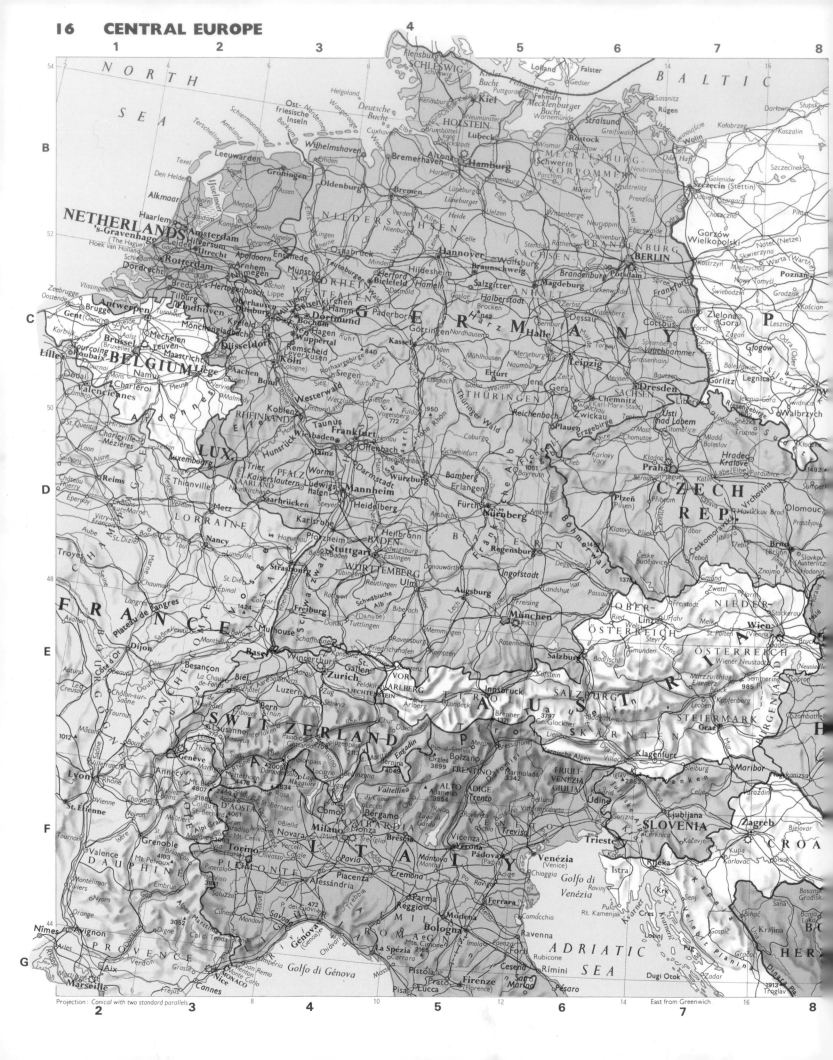

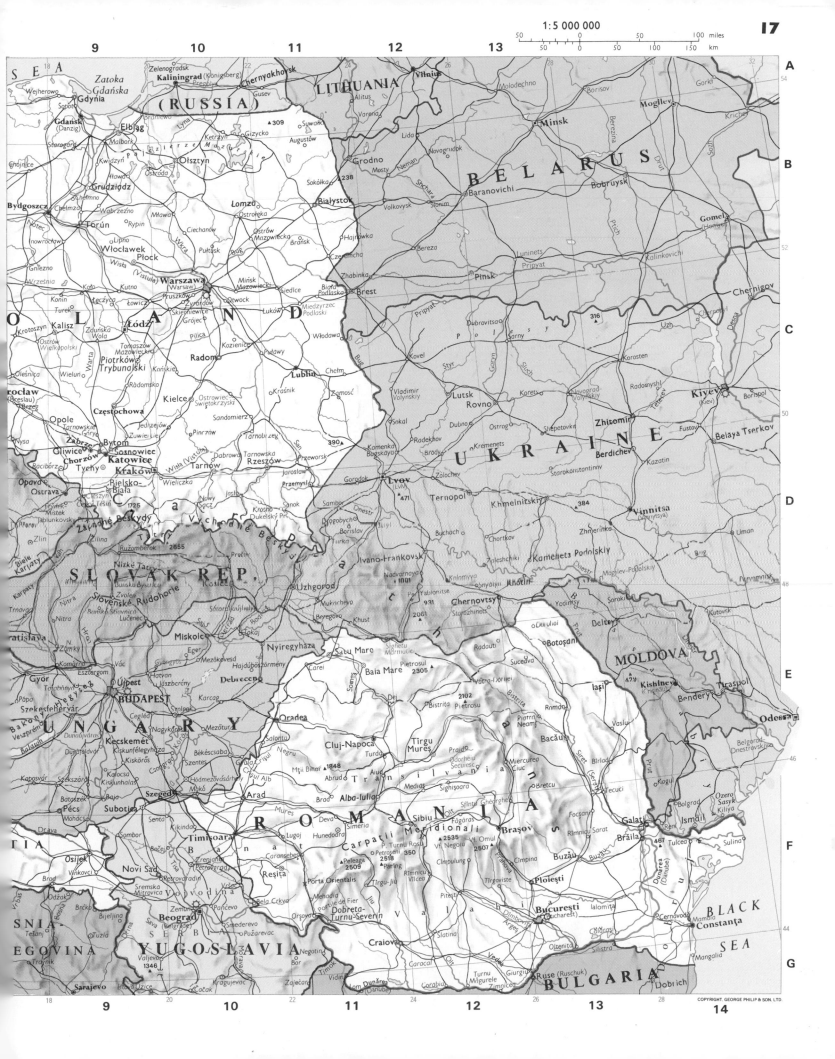

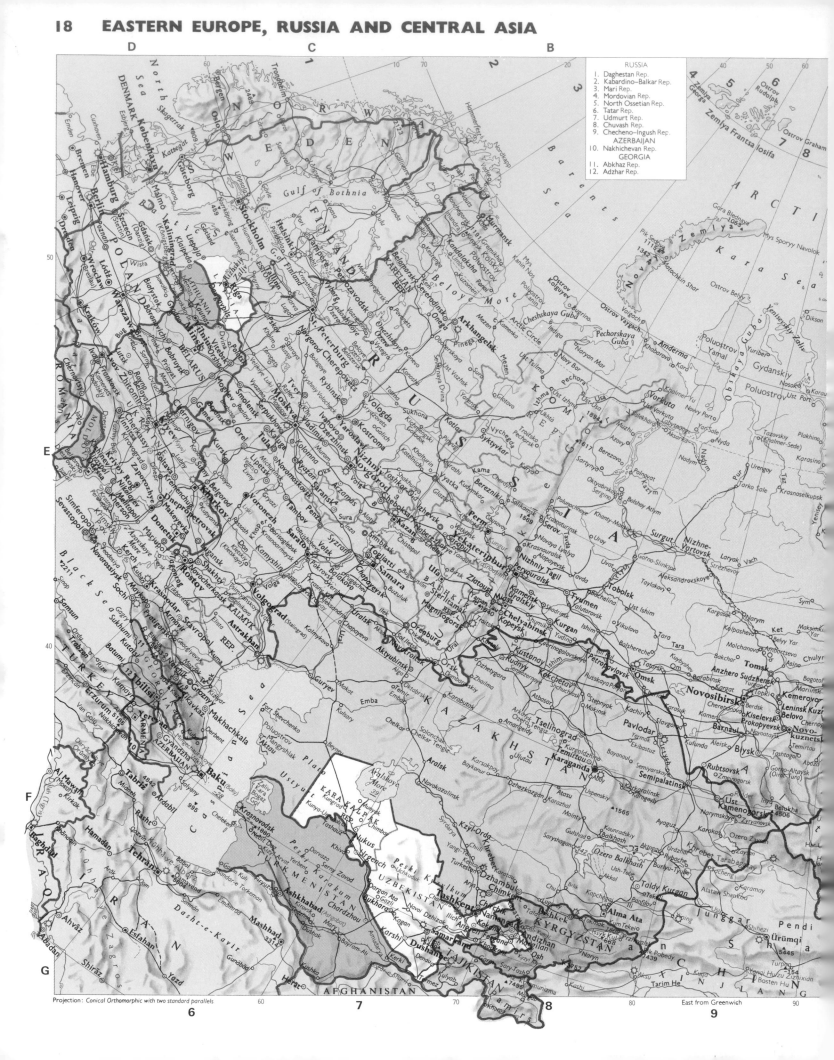

RUSSIA
1. Daghestan Rep.
2. Kabardino–Balkar Rep.
3. Mari Rep.
4. Mordovian Rep.
5. North Ossetian Rep.
6. Tatar Rep.
7. Udmurt Rep.
8. Chuvash Rep.
9. Checheno–Ingush Rep.
AZERBAIJAN
10. Nakhichevan Rep.
GEORGIA
11. Abkhaz Rep.
12. Adzhar Rep.

Projection: Conical Orthomorphic with two standard parallels

East from Greenwich

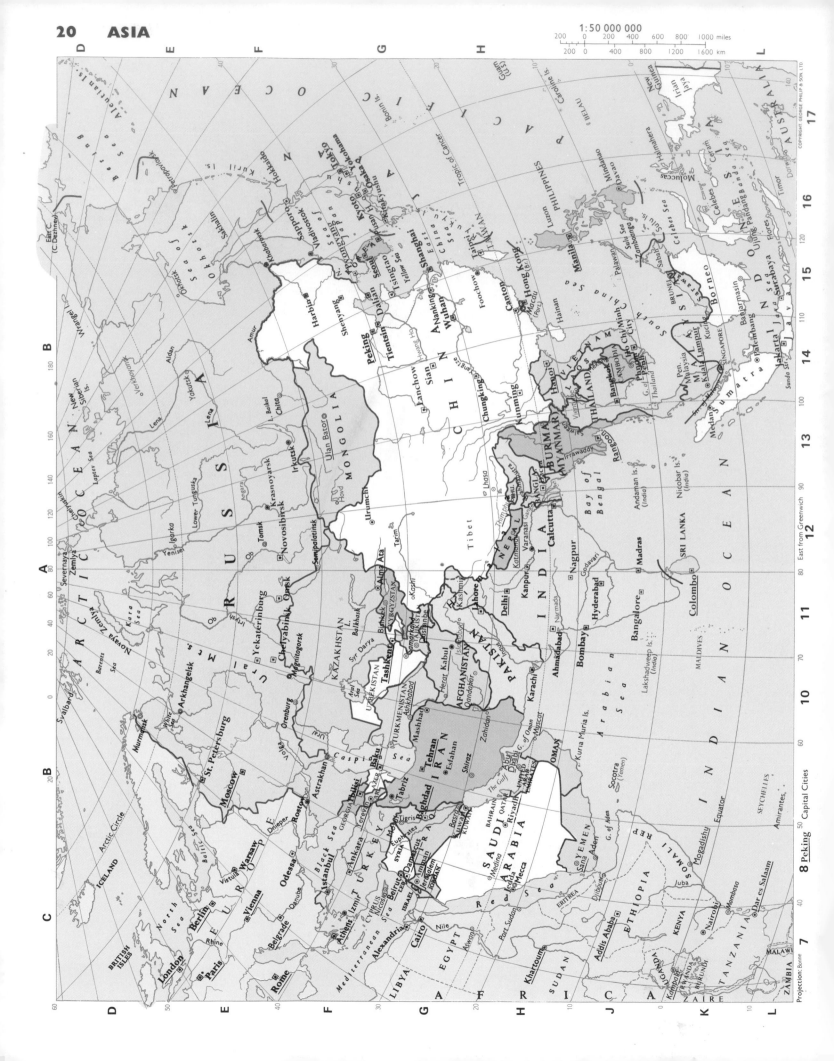

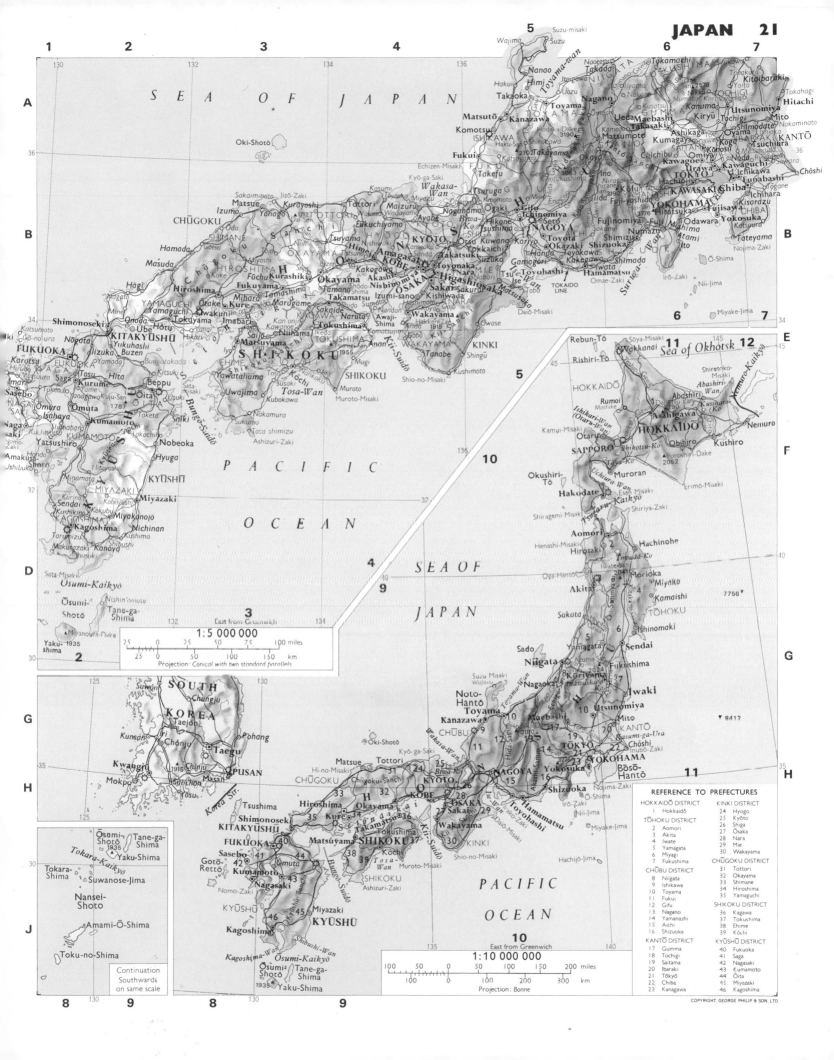

1:20 000 000

Projection: Bonne

East from Greenwich

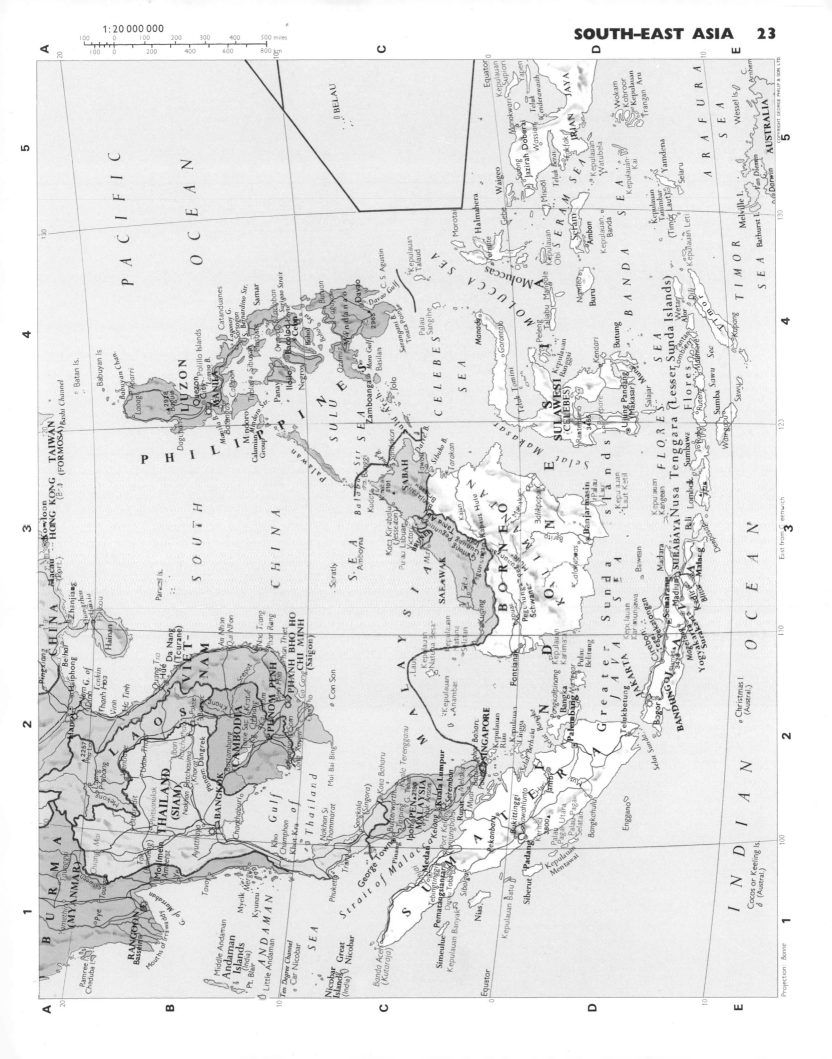

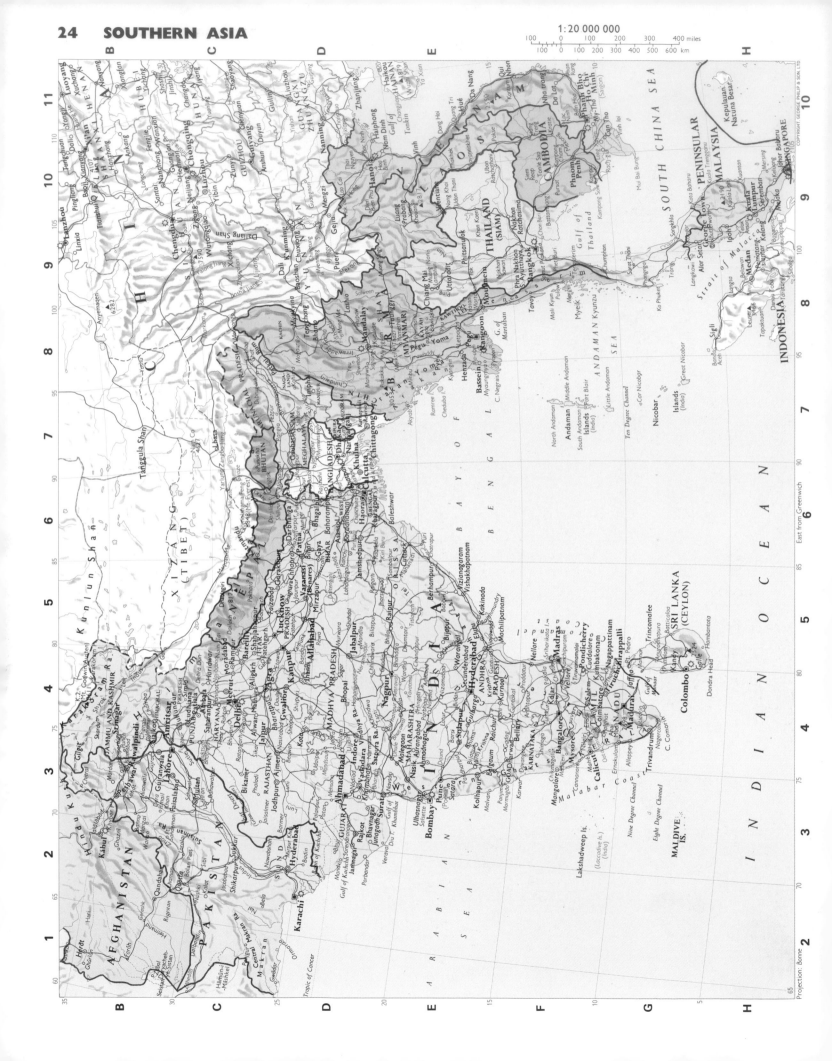

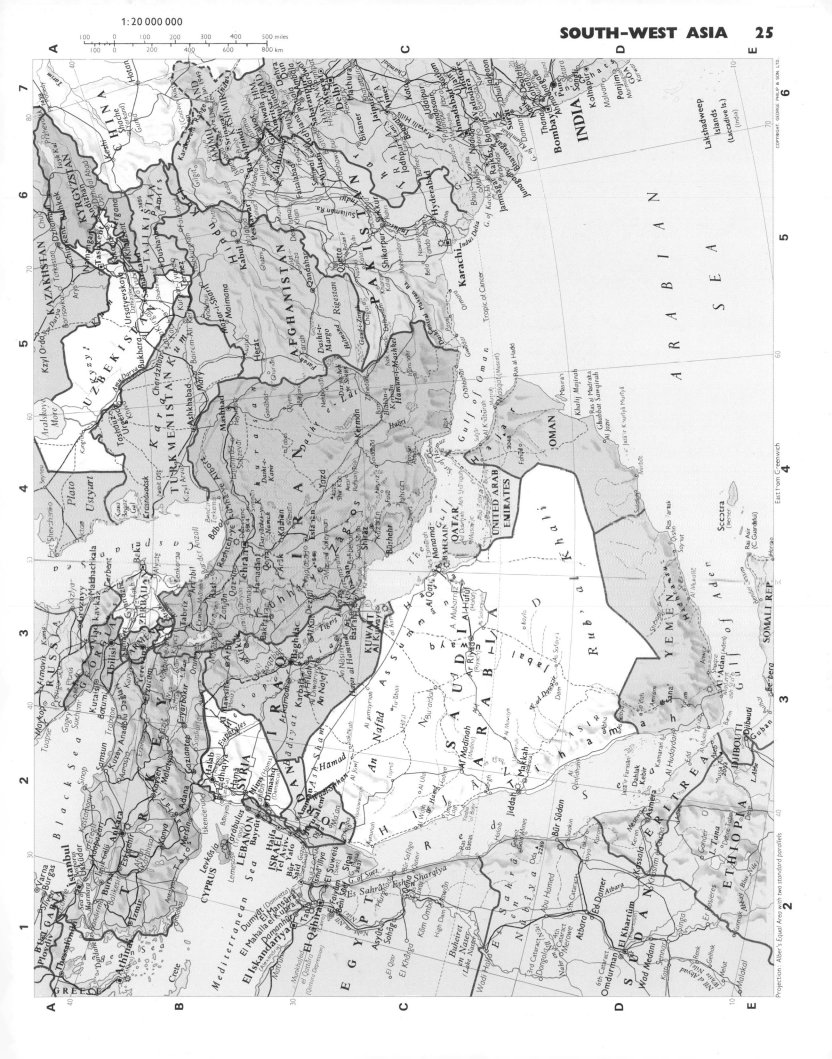

1:20 000 000

COPYRIGHT GEORGE PHILIP & SON, LTD.

East from Greenwich

Projection: Alber's Equal Area with two standard parallels

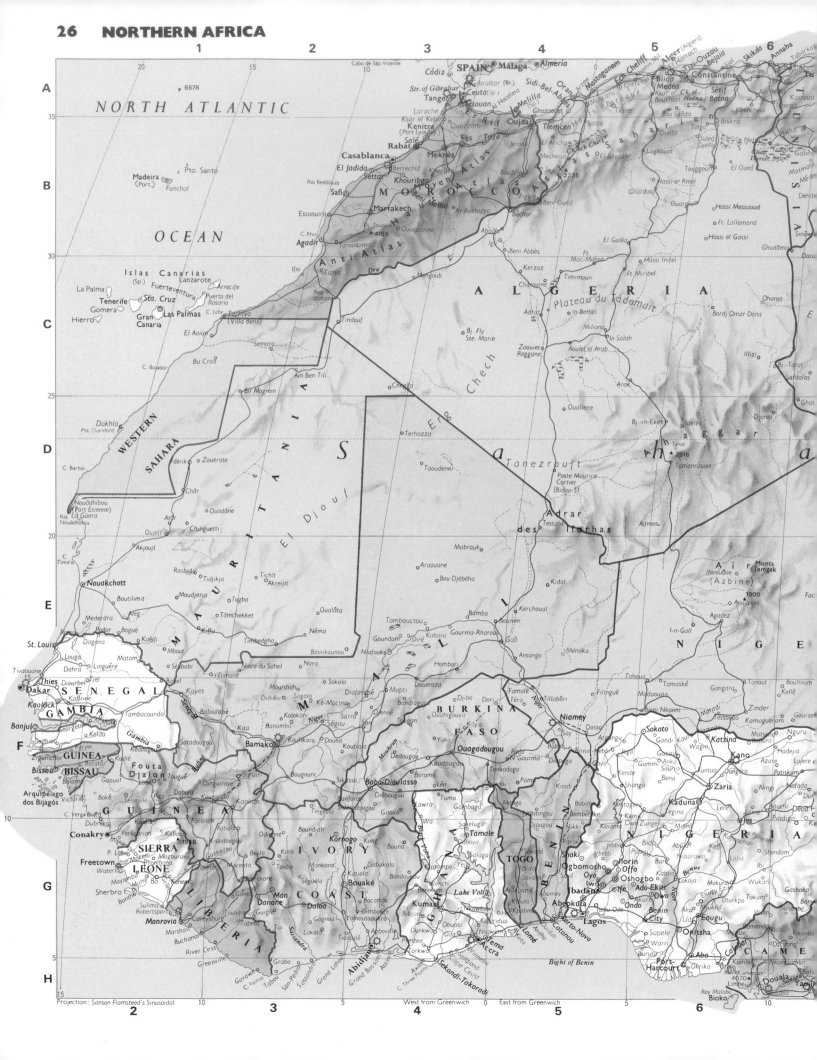

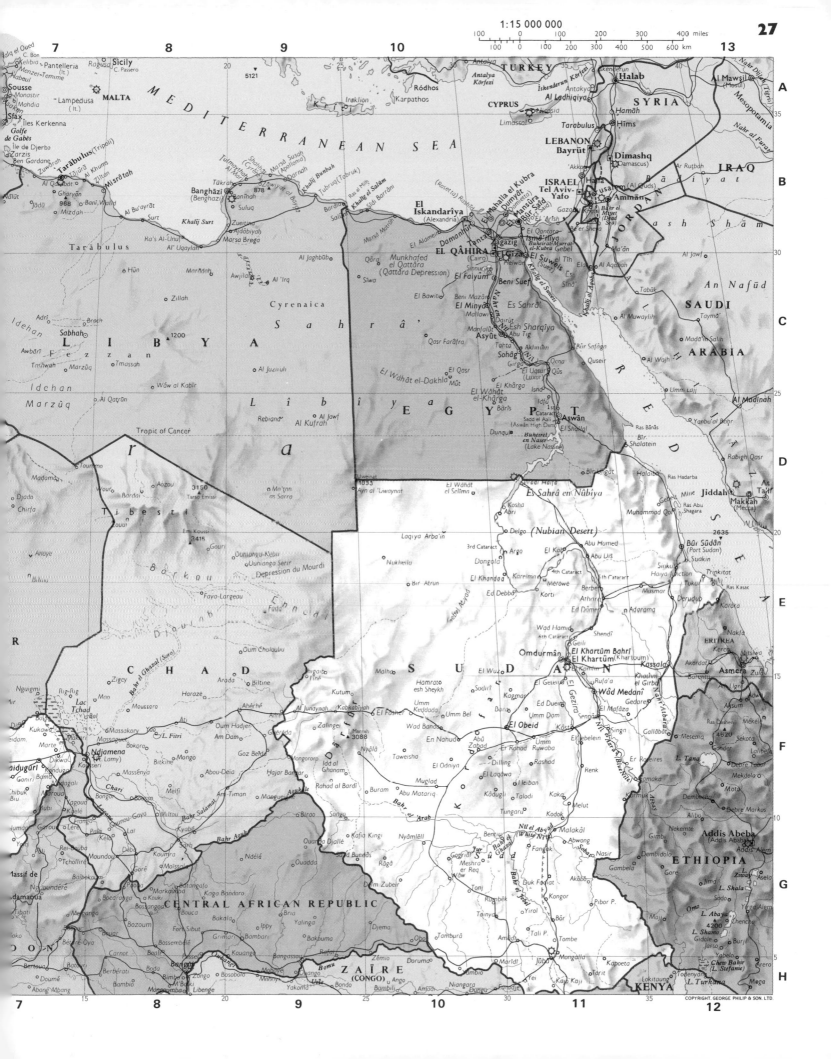

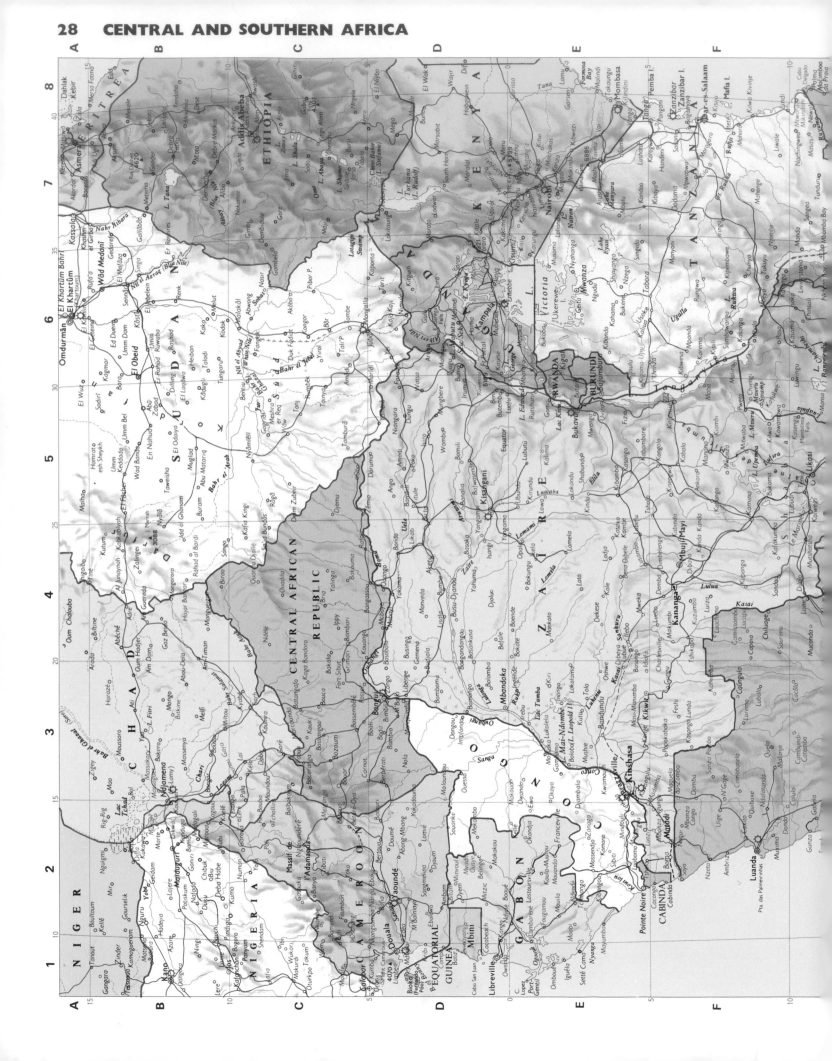

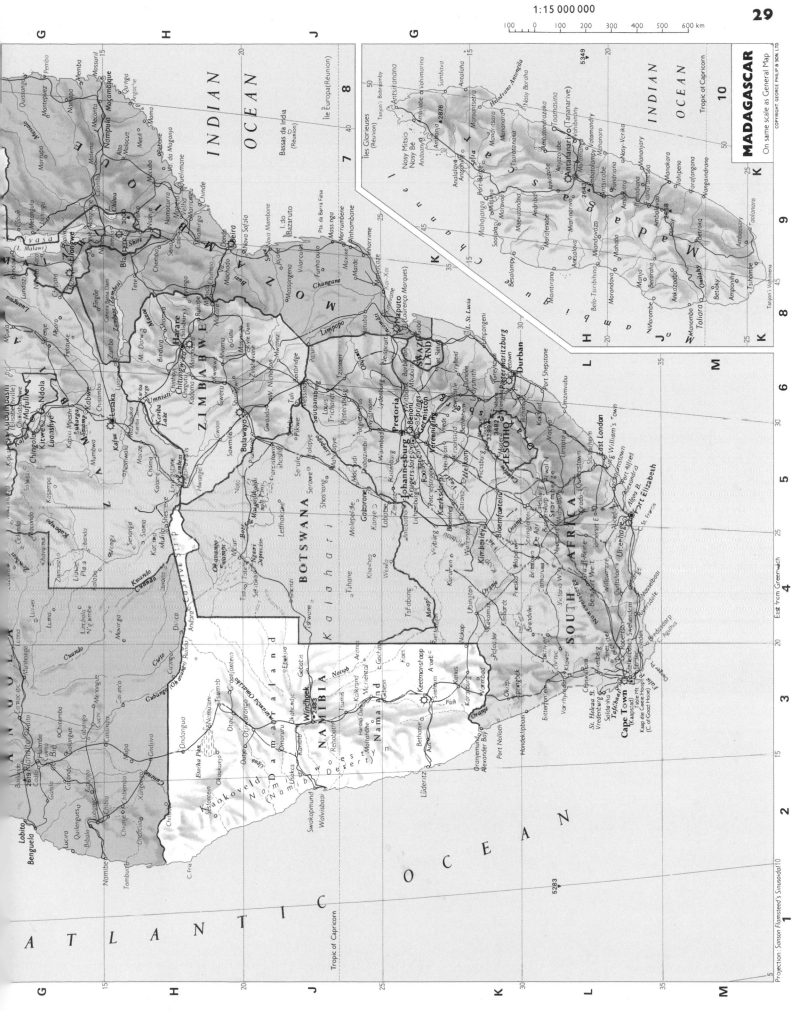

1:15 000 000

100   0   100   200   300   400   500   600 km

INDIAN OCEAN

INDIAN OCEAN

Tropic of Capricorn

MOZAMBIQUE

MALAWI
(L. Malawi)

ZIMBABWE

Harare (Salisbury)
Bulawayo

ZAMBIA

Lusaka

ANGOLA

NAMIBIA

Windhoek

BOTSWANA

Kalahari

Gaborone

SOUTH AFRICA

Pretoria
Johannesburg
Vereeniging
Kimberley
Bloemfontein

LESOTHO

SWAZILAND

Maputo (Lourenço Marques)

Durban
Pietermaritzburg

East London

Port Elizabeth

Cape Town (Kaapstad)

ATLANTIC OCEAN

Tropic of Capricorn

Projection: Sanson Flamsteed's Sinusoidal

East from Greenwich

Antananarivo (Tananarive)

INDIAN OCEAN

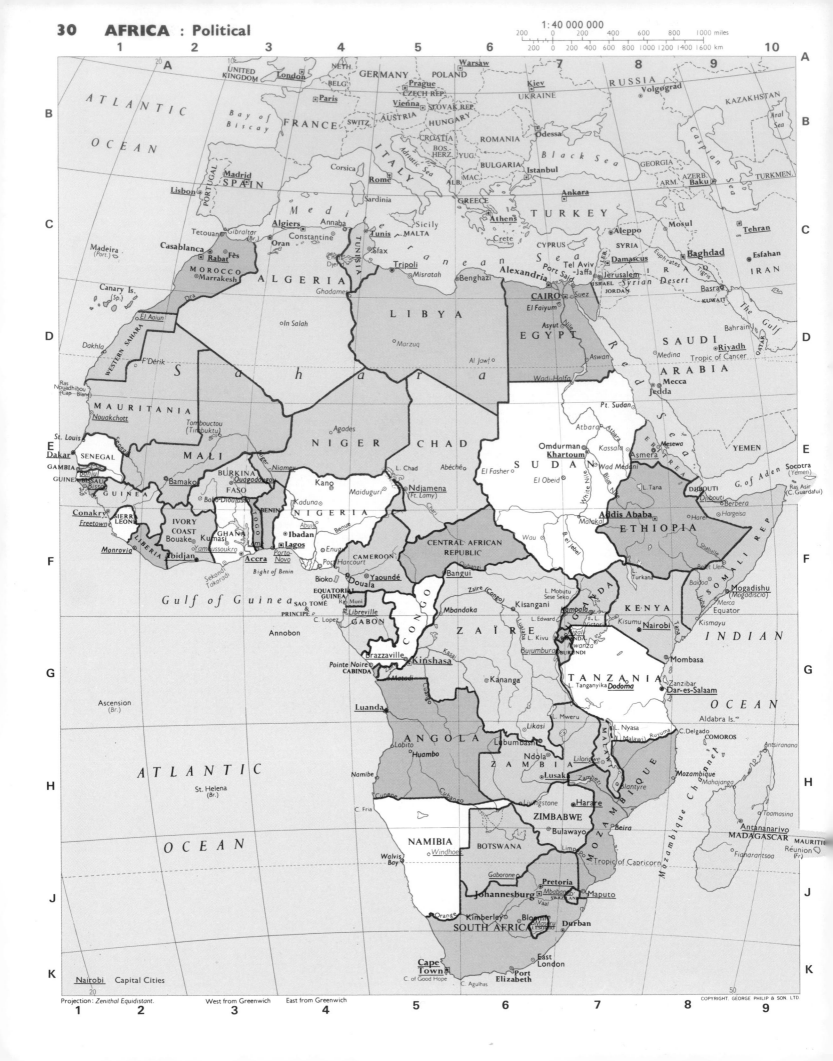

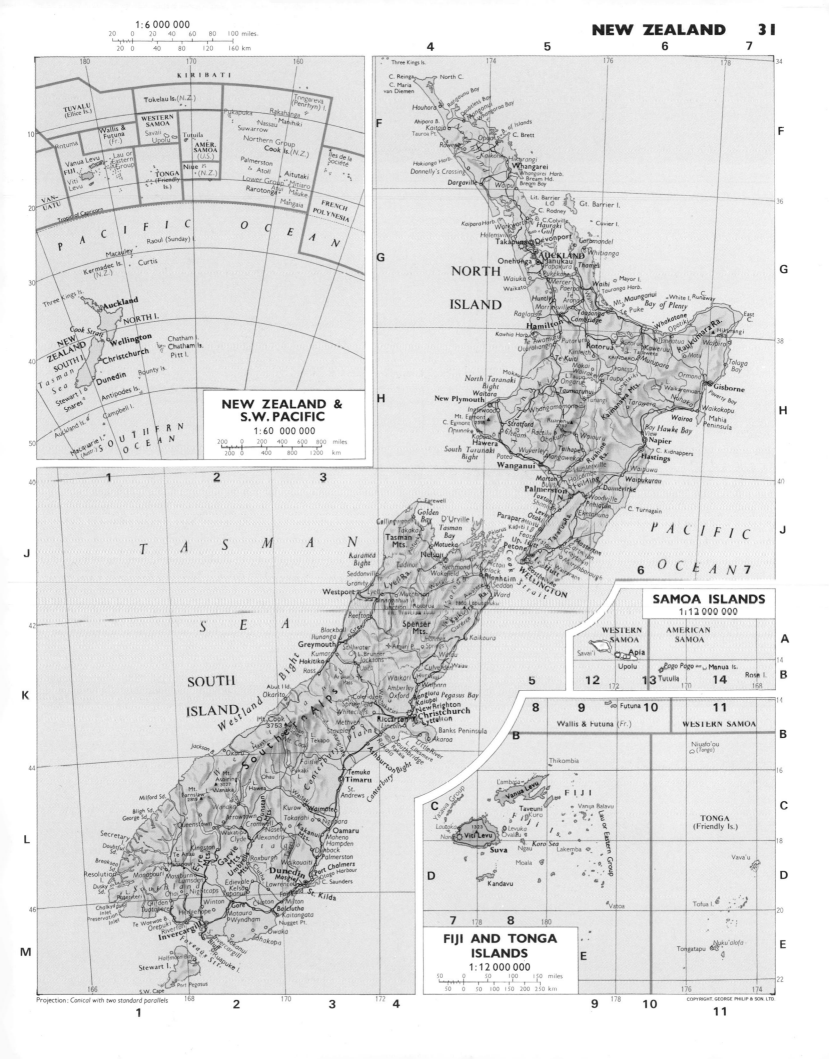

NEW ZEALAND & S.W. PACIFIC
1:60 000 000

SAMOA ISLANDS
1:12 000 000

FIJI AND TONGA ISLANDS
1:12 000 000

1:6 000 000

Projection: Conical with two standard parallels

COPYRIGHT. GEORGE PHILIP & SON. LTD.

HAWAII
1:10 000 000

Projection: Albers' Equal Area with two standard parallels

West from Greenwich

Projection: Sanson-Flamsteed's Sinusoidal

West fron

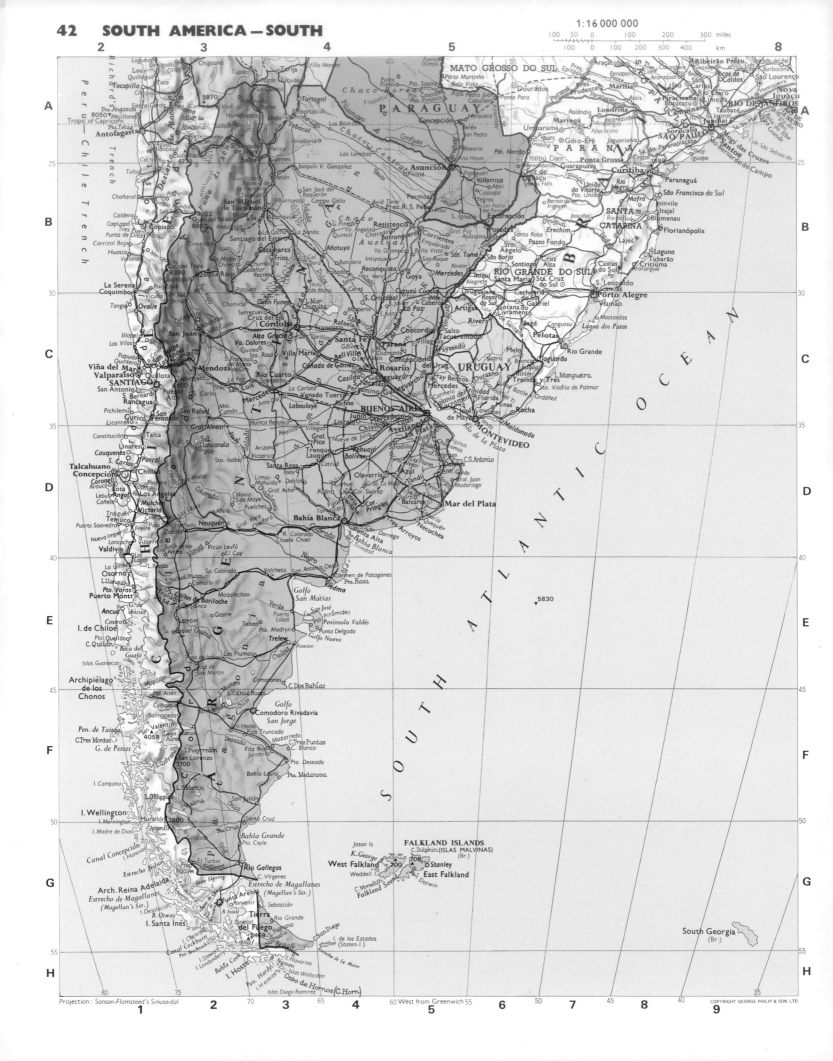

INDEX

The index contains the names of all the principal places and features shown on the maps. Each name is followed by an additional entry in italics giving the country or region within which it is located.

Physical features composed of a proper name (Erie) and a description (Lake) are positioned alphabetically by the proper name. The description is positioned after the proper name and is usually abbreviated.

The number in bold type which follows each name in the index refers to the number of the map page where that feature or place will be found. This is usually the largest scale at which the place or feature appears. The letter and figure which are in bold type immediately after the page number give the grid square on the map page, within which the feature is situated. The letter represents the latitude and the figure the longitude.

In some cases the feature itself may fall within the specified square, while the name is outside. This is usually the case only with features which are larger than a grid square. Rivers are indexed to their mouths or confluences, and carry the symbol ≈ after their names. A solid square ■ follows the name of a country, while an open square □ refers to a first order administrative area.

Abbreviations used in the index:

Afghan - Afghanistan
Arch. - Archipelago
Amer. - America
Atl. - Atlantic
B. - Bay
Bulg. - Bulgaria
C. - Cape
Cent. - Central
Chan. - Channel
Den. - Denmark
Dom. Rep. - Dominican Republic
Eq. - Equatorial
Fin. - Finland
G. - Gulf
Ger. - Germany
I(s). - Island(s), Isle(s)
Ind. - Indian
Ire. - Ireland
L. - Lake, Loch, Lough
Mong. - Mongolia
Mt(s). - Mount(s), Mountains(s)
N. - North
N.Z. - New Zealand
Neth. - Netherlands
Norw. - Norway
Pac. - Pakistan
Pen. - Peninsula
Port. - Portugal
Rep. - Republic
Rom. - Romania
S. - South
S. Arabia - Saudi Arabia
Str. - Strait
Swed. - Sweden
Switz. - Switzerland
U.A.E. - United Arab Emirates
U.K. - United Kingdom
U.S.A. - United States of America
W. - West
Yug. - Yugoslavia

A

Aachen, *Ger.* 16 C3
Aba, *Nigeria* 26 G6
Abadan, *Iran* 25 B3
Abashiri, *Japan* 21 F11
Abbeville, *France* 12 A4
Abeokuta, *Nigeria* 26 G5
Aberdare, *U.K.* 9 F4
Aberdeen, *U.K.* 10 D6
Aberystwyth, *U.K.* 9 E3
Abidjan, *Ivory Coast* 26 G4
Abilene, *U.S.A.* 36 D7
Abruzzi, □ *Italy* 14 C5
Abu Dhabi, *U.A.E.* 25 C4
Acapulco, *Mexico* 38 D5
Accra, *Ghana* 26 G4
Achill I., *Ire.* 11 C1
Aconcagua, *Argentina* 42 C3
Acre, □ *Brazil* 40 E4
Adamaoua, Massif de l', *Cameroon* 28 C2
Adana, *Turkey* 25 B2
Addis Abeba, *Ethiopia* 28 C7
Adelaide, *Australia* 33 E6
Aden, Gulf of, *Asia* 25 D3
Adriatic Sea, *Italy* 14 C6
Ægean Sea, *Greece* 15 E11
Afghanistan, ■ *Asia* 25 B5
Africa 30
Agadir, *Morocco* 20 D3
Agra, *India* 24 C4
Aguascalientes, *Mexico* 38 C4
Ahaggar, *Algeria* 26 D6
Ahmadabad, *India* 24 D3
Ahvāz, *Iran* 25 B3
Airdrie, *U.K.* 10 F5
Ajaccio, *France* 14 D3
Akershus, *Norw.* 7 F11
Akita, *Japan* 21 G11
Akron, *U.S.A.* 37 B10
Akureyri, *Iceland* 6 D4
Al 'Adan, *Yemen* 25 D3
Al Basrah, *Iraq* 25 B3
Al Hillah, *Iraq* 25 B3
Al Hufūf, *S. Arabia* 25 C3
Al Kut, *Iraq* 25 B3
Al Kuwayt, *Kuwait* 25 C3
Al Madinah, *S. Arabia* 25 C2
Al Manamāh, *S. Arabia* 25 C4
Al Mawsil, *Iraq* 25 B3
Al Qatif, *S. Arabia* 25 C3
Alabama, □ *U.S.A.* 37 D9
Alagôas, □ *Brazil* 41 E11
Alagoinhas, *Brazil* 41 F11
Aland, *Fin.* 7 F16
Alaska, □ *U.S.A.* 34 B4
Alba Iulia, *Rom.* 17 E11
Albacete, *Spain* 13 C5
Albania, ■ *Europe* 15 D9
Albany, *U.S.A.* 37 B12
Alberta, □ *Canada* 34 C8
Ålborg, *Den.* 7 H10
Albuquerque, *U.S.A.* 36 C5
Aldabra Is., *Africa* 30 F8
Alderney, *Channel Is.* 12 B2
Aldershot, *U.K.* 9 F7
Aleppo = Halab, *Syria* 25 B2
Alessándria, *Italy* 14 B3
Alesund, *Norw.* 6 E9
Aleutian Is., *U.S.A.* 34 C2
Alexandria = El Iskandarîya, *Egypt* 27 B10
Alfreton, *U.K.* 8 D6
Algarve, □ *Port.* 13 D1
Alger, *Algeria* 26 A5
Algeria, ■ *Africa* 26 C5
Algiers = Alger, *Algeria* 26 A5
Alicante, *Spain* 13 C5
Alice Springs, *Australia* 32 C5
Alkmaar, *Neth.* 16 B2
Allahabad, *India* 24 C5
Allentown, *U.S.A.* 37 B11
Alloa, *U.K.* 10 E5
Alma Ata, *Kazakhstan* 18 E8
Almeria, *Spain* 13 D4
Alps, *Europe* 12 D7
Alsace, □ *France* 12 B7
Altona, *Ger.* 16 B4
Älvsborg, □ *Swed.* 7 G12
Amagasaki, *Japan* 21 B4
Amapá, □ *Brazil* 41 C8
Amarillo, *U.S.A.* 36 C6
Amazonas, ≈ *S. Amer.* 41 D8
Amazonas, □ *Brazil* 40 D5
Amiens, *France* 12 B5
Ammān, *Jordan* 25 B2
Amritsar, *India* 24 B3
Amsterdam, *Neth.* 16 B2
Amundsen Gulf, *Canada* 34 A7
An Najaf, *Iraq* 25 B3
Anaheim, *U.S.A.* 36 D3
Anápolis, *Brazil* 41 G9
Anchorage, *Alaska* 34 B5
Ancohuma, *Bolivia* 40 G5
Ancona, *Italy* 14 C5
Andalucía, □ *Spain* 13 D3
Andaman Is., *India* 24 F7
Andes, Cord. de los, *S. Amer.* 40 G4
Andhra Pradesh, □ *India* 24 E4
Andorra, ■ *Europe* 13 A6
Andria, *Italy* 14 D7
Andros, *Greece* 15 F11
Andros I., *W. Indies* 39 C9
Angers, *France* 12 C3
Anglesey, *U.K.* 8 D3
Angola, ■ *Africa* 29 G3
Angoulême, *France* 12 D4
Angoumois, □ *France* 12 D3
Anguilla, *W. Indies* 38 J19
Anjou, □ *France* 12 C3
Ankara, *Turkey* 25 B2
Annaba, *Algeria* 26 A6
Anshan, *China* 22 B7
Antananarivo, *Madagascar* 29 H9
Antarctica 4 24C
Anticosti, Î. d', *Canada* 35 D13
Antigua & Barbuda, ■ *W. Indies* 38 K20
Antofagasta, *Chile* 42 A2
Antrim, *U.K.* 11 B5
Antwerpen, *Belgium* 16 C2
Aomori, *Japan* 21 F11
Apeldoorn, *Neth.* 16 B2
Appalachian Mts., *U.S.A.* 37 C10
Appennini, *Italy* 14 C5
Ar Ramadi, *Iraq* 25 B3
Ar Riyād, *S. Arabia* 25 C3
Arabian Sea, *Asia* 25 D5
Aracajú, *Brazil* 41 F11
Arad, *Rom.* 17 E10
Aragon, □ *Spain* 13 B5
Arāk, *Iran* 25 B3
Aral Sea = Aralskoye More, *Asia* 18 E6
Aralskoye More, *Asia* 18 E6
Arbil, *Iraq* 25 B3
Arbroath, *U.K.* 10 E6
Arctic Ocean, 4 12A
Ardabil, *Iran* 25 B3
Ardennes, *Belgium* 16 C2
Ardgour, *U.K.* 10 E3
Arenal, *Spain* 13 C7
Arequipa, *Peru* 40 G4
Argentina, ■ *S. Amer.* 42 E3
Århus, *Den.* 7 H11
Arizona, □ *U.S.A.* 36 D4
Arkansas, ≈ *U.S.A.* 37 C7
Arkansas, □ *U.S.A.* 37 D8
Arkhangelsk, *Russia* 18 C5
Arklow, *Ire.* 11 D5
Armagh, *U.K.* 11 B5
Armenia, ■ *Asia* 18 E5
Armenia, *Colombia* 40 C3
Arnhem, *Neth.* 16 C2
Arnhem Land, *Australia* 32 A5
Arran, *U.K.* 10 F3
Artois, □ *France* 12 A5
Aru Is., *Indonesia* 23 D5
Arunachal Pradesh, □ *India* 24 C7
Asahikawa, *Japan* 21 F11
Ascension, *Atl. Ocean* 30 F2
Ascoli Piceno, *Italy* 14 C5
Ashkhabad, *Turkmenistan* 18 F6
Asmera, *Eritrea* 28 A7
Assam □ *India* 24 C7
Astrakhan, *Russia* 18 E5
Asturias, □ *Spain* 13 A2
Asunción, *Paraguay* 42 B5
Aswân, *Egypt* 27 D11
Asyût, *Egypt* 27 C11
Athabasca, L., *Canada* 34 C9
Athens = Athínai, *Greece* 15 F10
Athínai, *Greece* 15 F10
Athlone, *Ire.* 11 C4
Atlanta, *U.S.A.* 37 D10
Atlantic Ocean 2 C7
Auckland, *N.Z.* 31 G5
Augsburg, *Ger.* 16 D5
Augusta, *U.S.A.* 37 D10
Aust-Agder, □ *Norw.* 7 G9
Austin, *U.S.A.* 36 D7
Australia, ■ *Australasia* 32
Australian Alps, *Australia* 33 F8
Australian Capital Territory, □ *Australia* 33 F8
Austria, ■ *Europe* 16 E6
Auvergne, □ *France* 12 D5
Avellaneda, *Argentina* 42 C5
Aviemore, *U.K.* 10 D5
Avignon, *France* 12 D6
Avila, *Spain* 13 B3
Avon, □ *U.K.* 9 F5
Ayers Rock, *Australia* 32 D5
Ayr, *U.K.* 10 F4
Azerbaijan, ■ *Asia* 18 E5
Azores, *Atl. Ocean* 2 C8
Azovskoye More, *Ukraine* 18 E4

B

Bābol, *Iran* 25 B4
Bacău, *Rom.* 17 E13
Bacabal, *Brazil* 41 D10
Badajoz, *Spain* 13 C2
Badalona, *Spain* 13 B7
Baden-Württemberg, □ *Ger.* 16 D4
Badenoch, *U.K.* 10 E4
Baffin Bay, *N. Amer.* 35 A13
Baffin I., *Canada* 35 B12
Baghdād, *Iraq* 25 B3
Bahamas, ■ *W. Indies* 39 C9
Bahia, □ *Brazil* 41 F10
Bahía Blanca, *Argentina* 42 D4
Bahrain, ■ *Asia* 25 C4
Baidoa, *Somalia* 30 F8
Baja California, □ *Mexico* 38 B2
Bakersfield, *U.S.A.* 36 C3
Bakhtaran, *Iran* 25 B3
Baku, *Azerbaijan* 18 E5
Balboa, *Panama* 38 H14
Baleares, Is., *Spain* 13 C6
Bali, *Indonesia* 23 D3
Balkhash, Ozero, *Kazakhstan* 18 E8
Ballarat, *Australia* 33 F7
Ballater, *U.K.* 10 D5
Ballymena, □ *U.K.* 11 B5
Ballymoney, □ *U.K.* 11 A5
Balmoral, *U.K.* 10 D5
Baltic Sea, *Europe* 7 H15
Baltimore, *U.S.A.* 37 C11
Bamako, *Mali* 26 F3
Bamberg, *Ger.* 16 D5
Banbridge, *U.K.* 11 B5
Bandon, *Ire.* 11 E3
Bandung, *Indonesia* 23 D2
Banff, *U.K.* 10 D6
Bangalore, *India* 24 F4
Banghāzi, *Libya* 27 B8
Bangkok, *Thailand* 23 B2
Bangladesh, ■ *Asia* 24 D6
Bangor, *U.K.* 11 B6
Bangui, *Cent. Afr. Rep.* 28 D3
Banjarmasin, *Indonesia* 23 D3
Banks I., *Canada* 34 A7
Bantry, *Ire.* 11 E2
Baotou, *China* 22 B5
Baranof I., *Alaska* 34 C6
Barbados, ■ *W. Indies* 38 P22
Barbuda, *W. Indies* 38 K20
Barcelona, *Spain* 13 B7
Bardsey I., *U.K.* 8 F3
Bareilly, *India* 24 C4
Barents Sea, *Arctic* 18 B4
Bari, *Italy* 14 D7
Barkly Tableland, *Australia* 32 B6
Barletta, *Italy* 14 D7
Barnsley, *U.K.* 8 D6
Barquisimeto, *Venezuela* 40 A5
Barra, *U.K.* 10 E1
Barrancabermeja, *Colombia* 40 B4
Barranquilla, *Colombia* 40 A4
Barrow-in-Furness, *U.K.* 8 C4
Barry, *U.K.* 9 F4
Basel, *Switz.* 16 E3
Basildon, *U.K.* 9 F8
Basilicata, □ *Italy* 14 D6
Basingstoke, *U.K.* 9 F6
Bass Strait, *Australia* 33 F8
Basse Terre, *Guadeloupe* 38 L20
Bath, *U.K.* 9 F5
Baton Rouge, *U.S.A.* 37 D8
Bauru, *Brazil* 41 H9
Bayern, □ *Ger.* 16 D5
Baykal, Ozero, *Russia* 19 D11
Bayonne, *France* 12 E3
Bayrūt, *Lebanon* 25 B2
Beaujolais, *France* 12 C6
Beaumont, *U.S.A.* 37 D8
Bedford, *U.K.* 9 E7
Bedfordshire, □ *U.K.* 9 E7
Beijing, *China* 22 C6
Beira, *Mozambique* 29 H7
Belarus, ■ *Europe* 18 D3
Belcher Is., *Canada* 35 C12
Belém, *Brazil* 41 D9
Belet Uen, *Somalia* 30 F8
Belfast, *U.K.* 11 B6
Belgium, ■ *Europe* 16 C2
Belgrade = Beograd, *Yug.* 15 B9
Belize, ■ *Cent. Amer.* 38 D7
Belmopan, *Belize* 38 D7
Belo Horizonte, *Brazil* 41 G10
Beloye More, *Russia* 18 C4
Ben Nevis, *U.K.* 10 E4
Benares = Varanasi, *India* 24 C5
Benbecula, *U.K.* 10 D1
Bengal, B. of, *Ind. Ocean* 24 E6
Bengbu, *China* 22 C6
Benguela, *Angola* 29 G2
Beni Suef, *Egypt* 27 C11
Benidorm, *Spain* 13 C5
Benin, ■ *Africa* 26 G5
Benin, Bight of, *Africa* 26 H5
Benin City, *Nigeria* 26 G6
Benoni, *S. Africa* 29 K5
Benue, ≈ *Africa* 26 G6
Benxi, *China* 22 B7
Beograd, *Yug.* 15 B9
Bergamo, *Italy* 14 B3
Bergen, *Norw.* 7 F8
Bering Sea, *Arctic* 19 D17
Berkeley, *U.S.A.* 36 C2
Berkshire, □ *U.K.* 9 F6
Berlin, *Ger.* 16 B6
Bermuda, □ *Atl. Ocean* 39 A12
Bern, *Switz.* 16 E3
Berwick-upon-Tweed, *U.K.* 8 B6
Besançon, *France* 12 C7
Béziers, *France* 12 E5
Bhopal, *India* 24 D4
Bhutan, ■ *Asia* 24 C7
Białystok, *Poland* 17 B11
Biarritz, *France* 12 E3
Biel, *Switz.* 16 E3
Bielefeld, *Ger.* 16 B4
Bielsko-Biała, *Poland* 17 D9
Bihar, □ *India* 24 D6
Bijagos, Arquipélago dos, *Guinea-Bissau* 26 F1
Bilbao, *Spain* 13 A4
Billings, *U.S.A.* 36 A5
Bioko, *Eq. Guinea* 28 D1
Birkenhead, *U.K.* 8 D4
Birmingham, *U.K.* 9 E6
Birmingham, *U.S.A.* 37 D9
Biscay, B. of, *Europe* 12 D1
Bishkek, *Kyrgyzstan* 18 E8
Bishop Auckland, *U.K.* 8 C6
Bitola, *Macedonia* 15 D9
Biwa-Ko, *Japan* 21 B5
Black Sea, *Europe* 18 E4
Blackburn, *U.K.* 8 D5
Blackpool, *U.K.* 8 D4
Blanc, Mt., *France* 12 D7
Blantyre, *Malawi* 29 H7
Blaydon, *U.K.* 8 C6
Blekinge, □ *Swed.* 7 H13
Bloemfontein, *S. Africa* 29 K5
Blue Nile = Nîl el Azraq, ≈ *Africa* 27 E11
Blyth, *U.K.* 8 B6
Bobo-Dioulasso, *Burkina Faso* 26 F4
Bochum, *Ger.* 16 C3
Boden, *Swed.* 6 D16
Bodmin Moor, *U.K.* 9 G3
Boggeragh Mts., *Ire.* 11 D3
Bogotá, *Colombia* 40 C4
Böhmerwald, *Ger.* 16 D6
Bolivia, ■ *S. Amer.* 40 G5

Index

Bologna, *Italy* 14 B4
Bolton, *U.K.* 8 D5
Bombay, *India* 24 E3
Bonn, *Ger.* 16 C3
Boothia, Gulf of, *Canada* ...35 A11
Bootle, *U.K.* 8 D4
Borås, *Swed.* 7 H12
Bordeaux, *France* 12 D3
Borders, □ *U.K.* 10 F5
Borlänge, *Swed.* 7 F13
Borneo, □ *Indonesia* 23 C3
Bornholm, *Den.* 7 J13
Bosnia-Herzegovina, ■ *Europe* ...14 B7
Bosporus, *Turkey* 25 A1
Boston, *U.S.A.* 37 B12
Boston, *U.K.* 8 E7
Bothnia, G. of, *Scandinavia* ...6 E16
Botoşani, *Rom.* 17 E13
Botswana, ■ *Africa* 29 J4
Bouaké, *Ivory Coast* 26 G3
Boulogne, *France* 12 A4
Bourbonnais, □ *France* 12 C5
Bourges, *France* 12 C5
Bournemouth, *U.K.* 9 G6
Bowland, Forest of, *U.K.* 8 D5
Boyne, ≈ *Ire.* 11 C5
Brăila, *Rom.* 17 F13
Bradford, *U.K.* 8 D6
Braga, *Port.* 13 B1
Brahmaputra, ≈ *India* 24 C7
Brandenburg, *Ger.* 16 B6
Brantford, *Canada* 35 D11
Brasília, *Brazil* 41 G9
Braşov, *Rom.* 17 F12
Bratislava, *Slovak Rep.* 16 D8
Bratsk, *Russia* 19 D11
Braunschweig, *Ger.* 16 B5
Bray, ≈ *Ire.* 11 C5
Brazil, ■ *S. Amer.* 41 F8
Brazzaville, *Congo* 28 E3
Breadalbane, *U.K.* 10 E4
Brecon Beacons, *U.K.* 9 F4
Breda, *Neth.* 16 C2
Bremen, *Ger.* 16 B4
Bremerhaven, *Ger.* 16 B4
Brentwood, *U.K.* 9 F8
Bréscia, *Italy* 14 B4
Bressay, *U.K.* 10 A7
Brest, *France* 12 B1
Bretagne, □ *France* 12 B2
Bridgeport, *U.S.A.* 37 B12
Bridgetown, *Barbados* 38 P22
Bridgwater, *U.K.* 9 F4
Bridlington, *U.K.* 8 C7
Brighton, *U.K.* 9 G7
Bríndisi, *Italy* 15 D7
Brisbane, *Australia* 33 D9
Bristol, *U.K.* 9 F5
Bristol Channel, *U.K.* 9 F3
British Columbia, □ *Canada* ...34 C7
Brno, *Czech Rep.* 16 D8
Broads, The, *U.K.* 8 E9
Brooks Range, *Alaska* 34 B5
Brugge, *Belgium* 16 C1
Brunei, ■ *Asia* 23 C3
Brussel, *Belgium* 16 C2
Bruxelles = Brussel, *Belgium* ...16 C2
Bucaramanga, *Colombia* 40 B4
Buchan, *U.K.* 10 D6
Bucharest = Bucureşti, *Rom.* ...17 F13
Buckinghamshire, □ *U.K.* 9 F7
Bucureşti, *Rom.* 17 F13
Budapest, *Hungary* 17 E9
Buenaventura, *Colombia* 40 C3
Buenos Aires, *Argentina* 42 C5
Buffalo, *U.S.A.* 37 B11
Buga, *Colombia* 40 C3
Bujumbura, *Burundi* 28 E5
Bukavu, *Zaïre* 28 E5
Bulawayo, *Zimbabwe* 29 J5
Bulgaria, ■ *Europe* 15 C11
Bûr Saîd, *Egypt* 27 B11
Bûr Sûdân, *Sudan* 27 E12
Burgas, *Bulg.* 15 C12
Burgenland, □ *Austria* 16 E8
Burgos, *Spain* 13 A4
Burkina Faso, ■ *Africa* 26 F4
Burma, ■ *Asia* 24 D8
Bursa, *Turkey* 25 A1
Burton-on-Trent, *U.K.* 8 E6
Buru, *Indonesia* 23 D4
Burundi, ■ *Africa* 28 E5
Buskerud, □ *Norw.* 7 F10
Bute, *U.K.* 10 F3
Bydgoszcz, *Poland* 17 B8
Bylot I., *Canada* 35 A12
Bytom, *Poland* 17 C9

C

Cabimas, *Venezuela* 40 A4
Cabinda, □ *Angola* 28 F2
Cáceres, *Spain* 13 C2
Cádiz, *Spain* 13 D2
Caen, *France* 12 B3
Caernarfon B., *U.K.* 8 D3
Cágliari, *Italy* 14 E3
Caha Mts., *Ire.* 11 E2
Cairngorm Mts., *U.K.* 10 D5

Cairo = El Qâhira, *Egypt* 27 B11
Calabar, *Nigeria* 26 G6
Calabria, □ *Italy* 14 E7
Calais, *France* 12 A4
Calcutta, *India* 24 D6
Calgary, *Canada* 34 C8
Cali, *Colombia* 40 C3
Calicut, *India* 24 F4
California, □ *U.S.A.* 36 C2
Callao, *Peru* 40 F3
Caltanissetta, *Italy* 14 F5
Camagüey, *Cuba* 39 C9
Cambodia, ■ *Asia* 23 B2
Camborne, *U.K.* 9 G2
Cambrian Mts., *U.K.* 9 E4
Cambridge, *U.K.* 9 E8
Cambridgeshire, □ *U.K.* 9 E8
Camden, *U.S.A.* 37 C12
Cameroon, ■ *Africa* 28 C2
Cameroon, Mt., *Cameroon* 28 D1
Campania, □ *Italy* 14 D6
Campbeltown, *U.K.* 10 F3
Campeche, G. de, *Mexico* 38 D6
Campina Grande, *Brazil* 41 E11
Campinas, *Brazil* 41 H9
Campo Grande, *Brazil* 41 H8
Campos, *Brazil* 41 H10
Canada, ■ *N. Amer.* 34 C10
Canarias, Is., *Atl. Ocean* 26 C1
Canaveral, C., *U.S.A.* 37 E10
Canberra, *Australia* 33 F8
Cannes, *France* 12 E7
Canouan, *W. Indies* 38 Q20
Cantabria, □ *Spain* 13 A3
Canterbury, *U.K.* 9 F9
Canton = Guangzhou, *China* ...22 D6
Cantù, *Italy* 14 B4
Cape Town, *S. Africa* 29 L3
Cape York Pen., *Australia* 33 A7
Caprivi Strip, *Namibia* 29 H4
Caracas, *Venezuela* 40 A5
Caratinga, *Brazil* 41 G10
Cardiff, *U.K.* 9 F4
Cardigan B., *U.K.* 9 E3
Carlisle, *U.K.* 8 C5
Carlow, *Ire.* 11 D5
Carmarthen B., *U.K.* 9 F3
Carnegie, L., *Australia* 32 D3
Caroline Is., *Pac. Ocean* 3 D17
Carpathians, *Europe* 17 E12
Carpentaria, Gulf of, *Australia* ...33 A6
Carrara, *Italy* 14 B4
Carrickfergus, *U.K.* 11 B6
Cartagena, *Spain* 13 D5
Cartagena, *Colombia* 40 A3
Cartago, *Colombia* 40 C3
Caruaru, *Brazil* 41 E11
Carúpano, *Venezuela* 40 A6
Casablanca, *Morocco* 26 B3
Caspian Sea, *Asia* 18 E6
Castellón de la Plana, *Spain* ...13 C5
Castilla - La Mancha, □ *Spain* ...13 C3
Castilla y Leon, □ *Spain* 13 B3
Castries, *St. Lucia* 38 N21
Cataluña, □ *Spain* 13 B6
Catánia, *Italy* 14 F6
Catanzaro, *Italy* 14 E7
Cavan, □ *Ire.* 11 B4
Caviana, I., *Brazil* 41 C9
Ceara, □ *Brazil* 41 E11
Cebu, *Philippines* 23 B4
Cedar L., *Canada* 34 C10
Celebes Sea, *Asia* 23 C4
Celebes = Sulawesi, *Indonesia* ...23 D4
Central, □ *U.K.* 10 E4
Central African Rep., ■ *Africa* ...28 C4
Central America, *N. Amer.* 38 E7
Ceram, *Indonesia* 23 D4
Cerignola, *Italy* 14 D6
Ceylon = Sri Lanka, ■ *Asia* 24 G5
Chad, ■ *Africa* 27 E8
Champagne, □ *France* 12 B6
Chang, ≈ *China* 22 C7
Changchun, *China* 22 B7
Changsha, *China* 22 D6
Changzhou, *China* 22 C7
Channel Is., □ *U.K.* 12 B2
Charleston, *U.S.A.* 37 D10
Charlotte, *U.S.A.* 37 C10
Charlottenburg, *Ger.* 16 B6
Charlottetown, *Canada* 35 D13
Chatham, *U.K.* 9 F8
Chattanooga, *U.S.A.* 37 C9
Cheju Do, *S. Korea* 22 C7
Chelmsford, *U.K.* 9 F8
Cheltenham, *U.K.* 9 F5
Chelyabinsk, *Russia* 18 D7
Chemnitz, *Ger.* 16 C6
Chengdu, *China* 22 C5
Cheremkhovo, *Russia* 19 D11
Chesapeake B., *U.S.A.* 37 C11
Cheshire, □ *U.K.* 8 D5
Chester, *U.K.* 8 D5
Chesterfield, *U.K.* 8 D6
Cheviot Hills, *U.K.* 8 B5
Chiba, *Japan* 21 B7
Chicago, *U.S.A.* 37 B9
Chichagof I., *Alaska* 34 C6
Chiclayo, *Peru* 40 E3

Chihuahua, *Mexico* 38 B3
Chile, ■ *S. Amer.* 42 D2
Chiloe I. de, *Chile* 42 E2
Chiltern Hills, *U.K.* 9 F7
Chimborazo, *Ecuador* 40 D3
China, ■ *Asia* 22 C4
Chingola, *Zambia* 29 G5
Chişinau = Kishinev, *Moldova* ...18 E3
Chita, *Russia* 19 D12
Chittagong, *Bangladesh* 24 D7
Chongqing, *China* 22 D5
Chonos, Arch. de los, *Chile* ...42 E2
Chorzów, *Poland* 17 C9
Christchurch, *N.Z.* 31 K4
Christmas I., *Australia* 23 E2
Chukotskoye More, *Russia* 19 C19
Chungking = Chongqing, *China* ...22 D5
Ciénaga, *Colombia* 40 A4
Cienfuegos, *Cuba* 39 C8
Cincinnati, *U.S.A.* 37 C10
Ciudad Bolivar, *Venezuela* 40 B6
Ciudad Guayana, *Venezuela* ...40 B6
Ciudad Juárez, *Mexico* 38 A3
Ciudad Real, *Spain* 13 C4
Clacton, *U.K.* 9 F9
Clare, □ *Ire.* 11 D2
Cleethorpes, *U.K.* 8 D7
Clermont-Ferrand, *France* 12 D5
Cleveland, *U.S.A.* 37 B10
Cleveland, □ *U.K.* 8 C6
Clonmel, *Ire.* 11 D4
Cluj-Napoca, *Rom.* 17 E11
Clwyd, □ *U.K.* 8 D4
Clyde, ≈ *U.K.* 10 F5
Clyde, Firth of, *U.K.* 10 F3
Clydebank, *U.K.* 10 F4
Coalville, *U.K.* 8 E6
Coast Ranges, *U.S.A.* 36 C2
Coatbridge, *U.K.* 10 F4
Coats I., *Canada* 35 B11
Cobh, *Ire.* 11 E3
Cochabamba, *Bolivia* 40 G5
Cocos or Keeling Is., *Australia* ...23 E1
Coimbra, *Port.* 13 B1
Colchester, *U.K.* 9 F8
Coleraine, □ *U.K.* 11 A5
Coll, *U.K.* 10 E2
Cologne = Köln, *Ger.* 16 C3
Colombia, ■ *S. Amer.* 40 C4
Colombo, *Sri Lanka* 24 G5
Colón, *Panama* 38 H14
Colonsay, *U.K.* 10 E2
Colorado, □ *U.S.A.* 36 C5
Colorado, ≈ *U.S.A.* 36 D4
Colorado Springs, *U.S.A.* 36 C6
Columbia, ≈ *U.S.A.* 36 A2
Columbia, *U.S.A.* 37 D10
Columbus, Georgia, *U.S.A.* ...37 D10
Columbus, Ohio, *U.S.A.* 37 C10
Colwyn Bay, *U.K.* 8 D4
Comayagua ... Como, *Italy* ...14 B3
Comeragh Mts., *Ire.* 11 D4
Comoros, ■ *Africa* 30 G8
Conakry, *Guinea* 26 G2
Concepcion, *Chile* 42 D2
Congo, ■ *Africa* 28 E3
Congo = Zaïre, ≈ *Africa* 28 D4
Connacht, *Ire.* 11 C2
Connecticut, □ *U.S.A.* 37 B12
Connemara, *Ire.* 11 C2
Constanţa, *Rom.* 17 F14
Constantine, *Algeria* 26 A6
Cookstown, *U.K.* 11 B5
Cooper Creek, ≈ *Australia* 33 D6
Copenhagen = København, *Den.* ...7 J12
Córdoba, *Spain* 13 D3
Córdoba, *Argentina* 42 C4
Corfu = Kérkira, *Greece* 15 E8
Cork, *Ire.* 11 E3
Cornwall, □ *U.K.* 9 G3
Coronation Gulf, *Canada* 34 B8
Corpus Christi, *U.S.A.* 36 E7
Corse, *France* 14 C3
Corsica = Corse, *France* 14 C3
Corumba, *Brazil* 40 G7
Cosenza, *Italy* 14 E7
Costa Blanca, *Spain* 13 C5
Costa Brava, *Spain* 13 B7
Costa del Sol, *Spain* 13 D4
Costa Dorada, *Spain* 13 B7
Costa Rica, ■ *Cent. Amer.* 39 F8
Cote d'Ivoire = Ivory Coast,
   ■ *Africa* 26 G3
Cotonou, *Benin* 26 G5
Cotopaxi, *Ecuador* 40 D3
Cotswold Hills, *U.K.* 9 F6
Cottbus, *Ger.* 16 C7
Coventry, *U.K.* 9 E6
Cowbridge ... Cherbourg, *France* ...12 B3
Craiova, *Rom.* 17 F11
Crawley, *U.K.* 9 F7
Cremona, *Italy* 14 B4
Crete = Kriti, *Greece* 15 G11
Crewe, *U.K.* 8 D5
Croatia, ■ *Europe* 14 B6
Cromarty, *U.K.* 10 D4
Cuba, ■ *W. Indies* 39 C8
Cúcuta, *Colombia* 40 B4
Cuenca, *Ecuador* 40 D3
Cuenca, *Spain* 13 B4

Cuiaba, *Brazil* 41 G7
Cumaná, *Venezuela* 40 A6
Cumbernauld, *U.K.* 10 F4
Cumbria, □ *U.K.* 8 C5
Cumbrian Mts., *U.K.* 8 C4
Curaçao, *Neth. Ant.* 40 A5
Curitiba, *Brazil* 42 B7
Cúzco, *Peru* 40 F4
Cwmbran, *U.K.* 9 F4
Cyclades = Kikládhes, *Greece* ...15 F11
Cyprus, ■ *Asia* 25 B2
Czech Rep., ■ *Europe* 16 D7
Czestochowa, *Poland* 17 C9

D

Dakar, *Senegal* 26 F1
Dalian, *China* 22 C7
Dallas, *U.S.A.* 37 D7
Damaraland, *Namibia* 29 J3
Damascus = Dimashq, *Syria* ...25 B2
Dandong, *China* 22 B7
Danube = Dunarea, ≈ *Europe* ...17 F14
Dar-es-Salaam, *Tanzania* 28 F7
Dardanelles, *Turkey* 25 A1
Darién, G. del, *S. Amer.* 40 B3
Darling, ≈ *Australia* 33 E7
Darlington, *U.K.* 8 C6
Darmstadt, *Ger.* 16 D4
Dartmoor, *U.K.* 9 G4
Dartmouth, *Canada* 35 D13
Darwin, *Australia* 32 A5
Datong, *China* 22 B6
Davao, *Philippines* 23 C4
Davis Str., *N. Amer.* 35 B14
Dayton, *U.S.A.* 37 C10
Dead Sea, *Asia* 25 B2
Deal, *U.K.* 9 F9
Dean, Forest of, *U.K.* 9 F5
Debrecen, *Hungary* 17 E10
Delaware, □ *U.S.A.* 37 C11
Delhi, *India* 24 C4
Denmark, ■ *Europe* 7 J10
Denver, *U.S.A.* 36 C6
Derby, *U.K.* 8 E6
Derbyshire, □ *U.K.* 8 D6
Derryveagh Mts., *Ire.* 11 A4
Des Moines, *U.S.A.* 37 B8
Dessau, *Ger.* 16 C6
Detroit, *U.S.A.* 37 B10
Devon, □ *U.K.* 9 G4
Devon I., *Canada* 35 A11
Dezfûl, *Iran* 25 B3
Dhaka, *Bangladesh* 24 D7
Dhodhekanisos, *Greece* 15 F12
Dieppe, *France* 12 B4
Dijon, *France* 12 C6
Dimashq, *Syria* 25 B2
Dingle B., *Ire.* 11 D1
Dingwall, *U.K.* 10 D4
Disappointment, L., *Australia* ...32 C3
Diyarbakir, *Turkey* 25 B3
Djibouti, ■ *Africa* 30 D8
Djibouti, *Djibouti* 30 D8
Dnepropetrovsk, *Ukraine* 18 E4
Dolomiti, *Italy* 14 A4
Dominica, ■ *W. Indies* 38 M20
Dominican Rep., ■ *W. Indies* ...39 D10
Don, ≈ *Russia* 18 E5
Doncaster, *U.K.* 8 D6
Donegal, *Ire.* 11 B3
Donetsk, *Ukraine* 18 E4
Dordrecht, *Neth.* 16 C2
Dornoch, *U.K.* 10 D4
Dorset, □ *U.K.* 9 G5
Dortmund, *Ger.* 16 C3
Douala, *Cameroon* 28 D1
Douglas, *U.K.* 8 C3
Dounreay, *U.K.* 10 C5
Douro, ≈ *Port.* 13 B1
Dover, *U.K.* 9 F9
Dover, Str. of, *U.K.* 9 G9
Down, □ *U.K.* 11 B6
Drakensberg, *S. Africa* 29 K5
Drammen, *Norw.* 7 G11
Dresden, *Ger.* 16 C6
Drogheda, *Ire.* 11 C5
Dubrovnik, *Croatia* 15 C8
Dudley, *U.K.* 9 E5
Duisburg, *Ger.* 16 C3
Duluth, *U.S.A.* 37 A8
Dumbarton, *U.K.* 10 F4
Dumfries, *U.K.* 10 F5
Dumfries and Galloway, □ *U.K.* ...10 F5
Dumyât, *Egypt* 27 B11
Dun Laoghaire, *Ire.* 11 C5
Dunarea, ≈ *Europe* 17 F14
Dundalk, *Ire.* 11 B5
Dundee, *U.K.* 10 E6
Dunedin, *N.Z.* 31 L3
Dunfermline, *U.K.* 10 E5
Dungannon, *U.K.* 11 B5
Dungarvan, *Ire.* 11 D4
Dunkerque, *France* 12 A5
Durango, *Mexico* 38 C4
Durban, *S. Africa* 29 K6
Durham, *U.K.* 8 C6
Durham, □ *U.K.* 8 C6
Dushanbe, *Tajikistan* 18 F7
Düsseldorf, *Ger.* 16 C3

Dyfed, □ *U.K.* 9 E3

E

East China Sea, *Asia* 22 D7
East Kilbride, *U.K.* 10 F4
East London, *S. Africa* 29 L5
East Siberian Sea, *Arctic* 19 B17
East Sussex, □ *U.K.* 9 G8
Eastbourne, *U.K.* 9 G8
Easter Is., *Pac. Ocean* 2 F17
Eastleigh ... Ebbw Vale, *U.K.* ...9 F4
Ebro, ≈ *Spain* 13 B6
Ebbw Vale, *U.K.* 9 F4
Ech Cheliff, *Algeria* 26 A5
Ecuador, ■ *S. Amer.* 40 D3
Eday, *U.K.* 10 B6
Edinburgh, *U.K.* 10 F5
Edmonton, *Canada* 34 C8
Edward, L., *Africa* 28 E5
Egypt, ■ *Africa* 27 D10
Eifel, *Ger.* 16 C3
Eigg, *U.K.* 10 E2
Eighty Mile Beach, *Australia* ...32 B3
Eindhoven, *Neth.* 16 C2
El Faiyûm, *Egypt* 27 F14
El Ferrol, *Spain* 13 A1
El Gîza, *Egypt* 27 C11
El Iskandarîya, *Egypt* 27 B10
El Khartûm, *Sudan* 27 E11
El Mahalla el Kubra, *Egypt* 27 B11
El Mansûra, *Egypt* 27 B11
El Minyâ, *Egypt* 27 C11
El Obeid, *Sudan* 27 F11
El Paso, *U.S.A.* 36 D5
El Qâhira, *Egypt* 27 B11
El Salvador, ■ *Cent. Amer.* ...38 E7
El Suweis, *Egypt* 27 C11
Elba, *Italy* 14 C4
Elbe, ≈ *Ger.* 16 B4
Elblag, *Poland* 17 A9
Elburz Mts., *Iran* 25 B4
Elche, *Spain* 13 C5
Eleuthera I., *W. Indies* 39 B9
Elgin, *U.K.* 10 D5
Ellesmere Port, *U.K.* 8 D5
Emilia Romagna, □ *Italy* 14 B4
England, □ *U.K.* 9 E6
English Channel, *Europe* 9 G6
Ennis, *Ire.* 11 D3
Enniscorthy, *Ire.* 11 D5
Enschede, *Neth.* 16 B3
Enugu, *Nigeria* 26 G6
Equatorial Guinea, ■ *Africa* ...28 D1
Erawadi Myit, ≈ *Burma* 24 E8
Erfurt, *Ger.* 16 C5
Erie, L., *N. Amer.* 35 D11
Eritrea, ■ *Africa* 28 A7
Erzurum, *Turkey* 25 B3
Esbjerg, *Den.* 7 J10
Esfahân, *Iran* 25 B4
Eskilstuna, *Swed.* 7 G14
Eskisehir, *Turkey* 25 B2
Espírito Santo, □ *Brazil* 41 G10
Essen, *Ger.* 16 C3
Essex, □ *U.K.* 9 F8
Estonia, ■ *Europe* 18 D3
Ethiopia, ■ *Africa* 28 C7
Etna, Mt., *Italy* 14 F6
Euphrates, ≈ *Asia* 25 B3
Evansville, *U.S.A.* 37 C9
Everest, Mt., *Nepal* 24 C6
Everglades, *U.S.A.* 37 E10
Évora, *Port.* 13 C2
Évvoia, *Greece* 15 E11
Exeter, *U.K.* 9 G4
Exmoor, *U.K.* 9 F4
Extremadura, □ *Spain* 13 C2
Eyre, L., *Australia* 33 D6
Eyre Peninsula, *Australia* 32 E6

F

Fairbanks, *Alaska* 34 B5
Falkirk, *U.K.* 10 F5
Falkland Is, *Atl. Ocean* 42 G5
Fareham, *U.K.* 9 G6
Farnborough, *U.K.* 9 F7
Faroe Is., *Atl. Ocean* 5 C4
Feira de Santana, *Brazil* 41 F11
Fens, The, *U.K.* 8 E7
Fermanagh, □ *U.K.* 11 B4
Ferrara, *Italy* 14 B4
Fès, *Morocco* 26 B3
Fetlar, *U.K.* 10 A8
Fife, □ *U.K.* 10 E5
Fiji, ■ *Pac. Ocean* 31 C7
Finland, ■ *Europe* 6 C19
Finnmark, □ *Norw.* 6 B18
Firenze, *Italy* 14 C4
Flandre, *Belgium* 16 C1
Fleetwood, *U.K.* 8 D4
Flensburg, *Ger.* 16 A4
Flinders I., *Australia* 33 F8
Flint, *U.S.A.* 37 B10
Florence = Firenze, *Italy* 14 C4
Flores, *Indonesia* 23 D4
Florida, □ *U.S.A.* 37 E10
Fóggia, *Italy* 14 D6
Folkestone, *U.K.* 9 F9

...rt de France, Martinique ...38 N20
...rt Smith, U.S.A. ...37 C8
...rt Wayne, U.S.A. ...37 B9
...rt William, U.K. ...10 E3
...rt Worth, U.S.A. ...36 D7
...rtaleza, Brazil ...41 D11
...orth, Firth of, U.K. ...10 E6
...oula, U.K. ...10 A6
...xe Channel, Canada ...35 B11
...ance, Europe ...12 C4
...anche-Comte, France ...12 C6
...ankfurt am Main, Ger. ...16 C4
...ankfurt an der Oder, Ger. ...16 B7
...änkische Alb, Ger. ...16 D5
...aser I., Australia ...33 D9
...aserburgh, U.K. ...10 D6
...ederikshavn, Den. ...7 H11
...ederikstad, Norw. ...7 G11
...eetown, Sierra Leone ...26 G2
...eiburg, Ger. ...16 D3
...ench Guiana, S. Amer. ...41 C8
...esno, U.S.A. ...36 C3
...iuli Venezia Giulia, Italy ...14 A5
...ome, L., Australia ...33 E6
...unze – Bishkek, Kirghizia ...18 E8
...ji-San, Japan ...21 B6
...ukuoka, Japan ...21 C2
...ukushima, Japan ...21 G11
...unabashi, Japan ...21 B7
...urneaux Group, Australia ...33 G8
...ürth, Ger. ...16 D5
...ushun, China ...22 B7
...uzhou, China ...22 D6
...yn, Den. ...7 J11

G

...abon, Africa ...28 E2
...aborone, Botswana ...29 J5
...airdner, L., Australia ...32 E6
...alaţi, Rom. ...17 F14
...alapagos Is., Pac. Ocean ...2
...alashiels, U.K. ...10 F6
...alicia, Spain ...13 A1
...ällivare, Swed. ...0 C10
...alloway, U.K. ...10 G4
...alveston, U.S.A ...37 E8
...alway, Ire. ...11 C2
...ambia, Africa ...26 F1
...amboa, Panama ...38 H14
...anga, Ind./Bangla. ...24 C4
...anges = Ganga, Ind./Bangla. ...24 C4
...aoxiong, Taiwan ...22 D7
...arda, L. di, Italy ...14 B4
...ary, U.S.A. ...37 B9
...ascogne, France ...12 E3
...aspé, Pén de, Canada ...35 D13
...ateshead, U.K. ...8 C6
...atun, Panama ...38 H14
...ävle, Swed. ...7 F14
...avleborg, Swed. ...7 F14
...aza, Israel ...25 B2
...aziantep, Turkey ...25 B2
...dansk, Poland ...17 A9
...dynia, Poland ...17 A9
...eelong, Australia ...33 F7
...elsenkirchen, Ger. ...16 C3
...enève, Switz. ...16 E3
...enova, Italy ...14 B3
...eorge Town, Malaysia ...23 C2
...eorgetown, Guyana ...40 B7
...eorgia, Asia ...18 E5
...eorgia, U.S.A. ...37 D10
...era, Ger. ...16 C6
...ermany, Europe ...16 C5
...ermiston, S. Africa ...29 K5
...erona, Spain ...13 B7
...hana, Africa ...26 G4
...iant's Causeway, U.K. ...11 A5
...ibraltar, Europe ...13 D3
...ibson Desert, Australia ...32 C3
...ifu, Japan ...21 B5
...igha, U.K. ...10 F3
...ijón, Spain ...13 A3
...illingham, U.K. ...9 F8
...isborne, N.Z. ...31 H7
...jøvik, Norw. ...7 F11
...lasgow, U.K. ...10 F4
...lendale, U.S.A. ...36 D3
...lenrothes, U.K. ...10 E5
...liwice, Poland ...17 C9
...logów, Poland ...16 C8
...loucester, U.K. ...9 F5
...loucestershire, U.K. ...9 F5
...oa, India ...24 E3
...oiânia, Brazil ...41 G9
...oias, Brazil ...41 F9
...ood Hope, C. of, S. Africa ...29 L3
...orkiy = Nizhniy Novgorod, Russia ...18 D5
...örlitz, Ger. ...16 C7
...osport, U.K. ...9 G6
...öteborg, Swed. ...7 H11
...otland, Swed. ...7 H15
...ötaland, Swed. ...7 G12
...ozo, Malta ...14 F6
...rampian, U.K. ...10 D5
...rampian Highlands, U.K. ...10 E4
...ran Canaria, Canary Is. ...26 C1

Granada, Spain ...13 D4
Grand Bahama I., W. Indies ...39 B9
Grand Canyon, U.S.A. ...36 C4
Grand Cayman, W. Indies ...39 D8
Grand Rapids, U.S.A. ...37 B9
Grangemouth, U.K. ...10 E5
Grantham, U.K. ...8 E7
Gravesend, U.K. ...9 F8
Graz, Austria ...16 E7
Great Abaco I., W. Indies ...39 B9
Great Australian Bight, Australia ...32 C4
Great Barrier Reef, Australia ...33 B8
Great Bear L., Canada ...34 B7
Great Divide, Australia ...33 C8
Great Falls, U.S.A. ...36 A4
Great Inagua I., W. Indies ...39 C10
Great Salt Lake, U.S.A. ...36 B4
Great Sandy Desert, Australia ...32 C3
Great Slave L., Canada ...34 B8
Great Victoria Desert, Australia ...32 D4
Great Wall, The, China ...22 C5
Great Yarmouth, U.K. ...8 E9
Greater Antilles, W. Indies ...39 D9
Greater Manchester, U.K. ...8 D5
Greece, Europe ...15 E9
Green Bay, U.S.A. ...37 B9
Greenland, N. Amer. ...4 A9
Greenock, U.K. ...10 F4
Greensboro, U.S.A. ...37 C11
Grenada, W. Indies ...38 Q20
Grenoble, France ...12 D6
Gretna Green, U.K. ...10 F5
Grey Range, Australia ...33 D7
Grimsby, U.K. ...8 D7
Groningen, Neth. ...16 B3
Groot Karoo, S. Africa ...29 L4
Groote Eylandt, Australia ...33 A6
Gross Glockner, Austria ...16 E6
Grudziadz, Poland ...17 B9
Guadalajara, Mexico ...38 C4
Guadalajara, Spain ...13 B4
Guadarrama, Sierra de, Spain ...13 B4
Guadeloupe, W. Indies ...38 L20
Guadiana, Port. ...13 D2
Guadix, Spain ...13 D4
Guangzhou, China ...22 D6
Guantanamo, Cuba ...39 C9
Guatemala, Cent. Amer. ...38 D6
Guatemala City, Guatemala ...38 E6
Guayaquil, Ecuador ...40 D2
Guelph, Canada ...35 D11
Guernsey, Channel Is. ...12 B2
Guildford, U.K. ...9 F7
Guinea, Africa ...26 F2
Guinea-Bissau, Africa ...26 F1
Guiyang, China ...22 D5
Gujarat, India ...24 D3
Gulf, The, Asia ...25 C4
Guyana, S. Amer. ...40 B7
Guyenne, France ...12 D4
Gwalior, India ...24 C4
Gwent, U.K. ...9 F4
Gwynedd, U.K. ...8 E4

H

Haarlem, Neth. ...16 B2
Hachinohe, Japan ...21 F11
Hadrian's Wall, U.K. ...8 C5
Hagen, Ger. ...16 C3
Haifa, Israel ...25 B2
Hainan Dao, China ...22 E6
Haiti, W. Indies ...39 D10
Hakodate, Japan ...21 F11
Halab, Syria ...25 B2
Halberstadt, Ger. ...16 C5
Halifax, Canada ...35 D13
Halifax, U.K. ...8 D6
Halland, Swed. ...7 H12
Halle, Ger. ...16 C5
Halmstad, Swed. ...7 H12
Hamã, Syria ...25 B2
Hamadān, Iran ...25 B3
Hamamatsu, Japan ...21 B5
Hamar, Norw. ...7 F11
Hamburg, Ger. ...16 B5
Hame, Fin. ...7 F17
Hameln, Ger. ...16 B4
Hamilton, N.Z. ...31 G5
Hamilton, U.K. ...10 F4
Hamilton, Canada ...35 D11
Hamm, Ger. ...16 C3
Hammerfest, Norw. ...6 A17
Hammond, U.S.A. ...37 B9
Hampshire, U.K. ...9 F6
Hangzhou, China ...22 C6
Hannover, Ger. ...16 B4
Hanoi, Vietnam ...23 A2
Harare, Zimbabwe ...29 H6
Harbin, China ...22 B7
Hargeisa, Somalia ...30 F8
Harlow, U.K. ...9 F8
Härnösand, Swed. ...6 E15
Harrogate, U.K. ...8 D6
Hartlepool, U.K. ...8 C6
Haryana, India ...24 C3
Hastings, N.Z. ...31 H6
Hastings, U.K. ...9 G8

Haugesund, Norw. ...7 G8
Haut Atlas, Morocco ...26 B4
Havana = La Habana, Cuba ...39 C8
Havant, U.K. ...9 G7
Hawaii, Pac. Ocean ...2 C2
Hawaii, U.S.A. ...36 H16
Hawick, U.K. ...10 F6
Hedmark, Norw. ...7 F11
Hefei, China ...22 C6
Heidelberg, Ger. ...16 D4
Heilbronn, Ger. ...16 D4
Helmsdale, U.K. ...10 C5
Helsingborg, Swed. ...7 H12
Helsingor, Den. ...7 H12
Helsinki, Fin. ...7 F18
Hemel Hempstead, U.K. ...9 F7
Hengyang, China ...22 D6
Herat, Afghan. ...25 B5
Hereford, U.K. ...9 E5
Hereford & Worcester, U.K. ...9 E5
Herford, Ger. ...16 B4
Hermosillo, Mexico ...38 B2
Hertfordshire, U.K. ...9 F7
Hessen, Ger. ...16 C4
Higashiōsaka, Japan ...21 B4
High Wycombe, U.K. ...9 F7
Highland, U.K. ...10 D4
Hildesheim, Ger. ...16 B4
Hilversum, Neth. ...16 B2
Himachal Pradesh, India ...24
Himalaya, Asia ...24 C5
Himeji, Japan ...21 B4
Hims, Syria ...25 B2
Hindu Kush, Afghan. ...24 B3
Hirosaki, Japan ...21 F11
Hiroshima, Japan ...21 B3
Hobart, Australia ...33 G8
Hohhot, China ...22 B6
Hokkaido, Japan ...21 F11
Holderness, U.K. ...8 D7
Holguin, Cuba ...39 C9
Hollywood, U.S.A. ...36 D3
Honduras, Cent. Amer. ...38 E7
Hønefoss, Norw. ...7 F11
Hong Kong, Asia ...22 D6
Honolulu, Hawaii ...36 H16
Honshu, Japan ...21 B4
Hordaland, Norw. ...7 F9
Hormuz, Str. of, Asia ...25 C4
Horn, C. = Hornos, C. de, Chile ...42 H3
Hornos, C. de, Chile ...42 H3
Horsens, Den. ...7 J10
Hospitalet, Spain ...13 B7
Houghton-le-Spring, U.K. ...8 C6
Houston, U.S.A. ...37 E7
Howrah, India ...24 D6
Hoy, U.K. ...10 C5
Hradec Kralove, Czech Rep. ...16 C7
Huainan, China ...22 C6
Huang, = China ...22 C6
Huascarán, Peru ...40 D2
Huddersfield, U.K. ...8 D6
Hudson Bay, Canada ...35 B11
Hudson Str., Canada ...35 B12
Huelva, Spain ...13 D2
Huesca, Spain ...13 A5
Hull, U.K. ...8 D7
Humber, U.K. ...8 D7
Humberside, U.K. ...8 D7
Hungary, Europe ...17 E9
Hunsrück, Ger. ...16 D3
Huron, L., N. Amer. ...37 B10
Hyderabad, India ...24 E4
Hyderabad, Pak. ...24 C2

I

Iaşi, Rom. ...17 E13
Ibadan, Nigeria ...26 G5
Ibagué, Colombia ...40 C3
Ibiza, Spain ...13 C6
Iceland, Europe ...6 D4
Ichinomiya, Japan ...21 B5
Idaho, U.S.A. ...36 B3
Ikaría, Greece ...15 F12
Île-de-France, France ...12 B5
Illinois, U.S.A. ...37 B9
Ilorin, Nigeria ...26 G5
Imphal, India ...24 D7
Inch'on, S. Korea ...22 C7
India, Asia ...24 E4
Indian Ocean ...24 H3
Indiana, U.S.A. ...37 C9
Indianapolis, U.S.A. ...37 C9
Indonesia, Asia ...23 D3
Indore, India ...24 D4
Indus, Pakistan ...24 C2
Ingolstadt, Ger. ...16 D5
Inishowen Pen., Ire. ...11 A4
Inner Hebrides, U.K. ...10 D2
Innsbruck, Austria ...16 E5
Invercargill, N.Z. ...31 M2
Invergordon, U.K. ...10 D4
Inverness, U.K. ...10 D4
Iona, U.K. ...10 E2
Ionian Sea, Europe ...15 E8
Iónioi Nisoi, Greece ...15 E9
Iowa, U.S.A. ...37 B8

Ípiros, Greece ...15 E9
Ipswich, U.K. ...9 E9
Iquique, Chile ...40 H4
Iquitos, Peru ...40 D4
Iran, Asia ...25 B4
Iraq, Asia ...25 B3
Ireland, Europe ...11 C4
Irian Jaya, Indonesia ...23 D5
Irish Sea, Europe ...8 D2
Irkutsk, Russia ...19 D11
Irrawady = Erawadi Myit, Burma ...24 E8
Irvine, U.K. ...10 F4
Islay, U.K. ...10 F2
Israel, Asia ...25 B2
Istanbul, Turkey ...25 A1
Italy, Europe ...14 C4
Ivory Coast, Africa ...26 G3
Iwaki, Japan ...21 G11
Iwo, Nigeria ...26 G5
Izmir, Turkey ...25 B1

J

Jabalpur, India ...24 D5
Jackson, U.S.A. ...37 D8
Jacksonville, U.S.A. ...37 D10
Jaén, Spain ...13 D4
Jaipur, India ...24 C4
Jakarta, Indonesia ...23 D2
Jamaica, W. Indies ...39 D9
James Bay, Canada ...35 C11
Jammu & Kashmir, India ...24 B3
Jämtland, Norw. ...6 E13
Japan, Asia ...21 G10
Japan, Sea of, Asia ...21 A3
Java, Indonesia ...23 D2
Jena, Ger. ...16 C5
Jerez, Spain ...13 D2
Jersey, Channel Is. ...12 B2
Jersey City, U.S.A. ...37 B12
Jerusalem, Israel ...25 B2
Jiddah, S. Arabia ...25 C2
Jilin, China ...22 B7
Jilong, Taiwan ...22 D7
Jinan, China ...22 C6
Jinzhou, China ...22 B7
João Pessoa, Brazil ...41 E12
Johannesburg, S. Africa ...29 K5
John O'Groats, U.K. ...10 C5
Johnstone, U.K. ...10 F4
Jönköping, Swed. ...7 H12
Jordan, Asia ...25 B2
Juàzeiro do Norte, Brazil ...41 E11
Juiz de Fora, Brazil ...41 H10
Jundiaí, Brazil ...42 A7
Jura, Europe ...12 C6
Jura, U.K. ...10 F3

K

Kabul, Afghan. ...25 B5
Kaduna, Nigeria ...26 F6
Kagoshima, Japan ...21 D2
Kaiserslautern, Ger. ...16 D3
Kalahari, Africa ...29 J4
Kalgoorlie, Australia ...32 F3
Kaliningrad, Russia ...18 D3
Kalisz, Poland ...17 C9
Kalmar, Swed. ...7 H14
Kamaishi, Japan ...21 G11
Kampala, Uganda ...28 D6
Kampuchea = Cambodia, Asia ...23 B2
Kananga, Zaïre ...28 F4
Kanazawa, Japan ...21 A5
Kandahar, Afghan. ...25 B5
Kangaroo I., Australia ...33 F6
Kano, Nigeria ...26 F6
Kanpur, India ...24 C5
Kansas, U.S.A. ...36 C7
Kansas City, U.S.A. ...37 C8
Kaokoveld, Namibia ...29 H2
Kaolack, Senegal ...26 F1
Kara Sea, Arctic ...18 B7
Karachi, Pak. ...24 D2
Karaganda, Kazakhstan ...18 E8
Karbalā, Iraq ...25 B3
Kariba L., Africa ...29 H5
Karlskrona, Swed. ...7 H13
Karlsruhe, Ger. ...16 D4
Karlstad, Swed. ...7 G12
Kärnten, Austria ...16 E6
Kárpathos, Greece ...15 G12
Kāshān, Iran ...25 B4
Kassel, Ger. ...16 C4
Katmandu, Nepal ...24 C6
Katowice, Poland ...17 C9
Katsina, Nigeria ...26 F6
Kattegat, Scandinavia ...7 H11
Kawaguchi, Japan ...21 B6
Kawasaki, Japan ...21 B6
Kayseri, Turkey ...25 B2
Kazakhstan, Asia ...18 E7
Kazan, Russia ...18 D5
Kecskemét, Hungary ...17 E9
Kefallinia, Greece ...15 E9
Keflavik, Iceland ...6 D2
Keighley, U.K. ...8 D6
Kemān, Iran ...25 B4
Kemi, Fin. ...6 D18

Kenitra, Morocco ...26 B3
Kent, U.K. ...9 F8
Kentucky, U.S.A. ...37 C9
Kenya, Africa ...28 D7
Kenya, Mt., Kenya ...28 E7
Kerala, India ...24 F4
Kérkira, Greece ...15 E8
Kerry, Ire. ...11 D2
Keski - Suomen, Fin. ...6 E18
Key West, U.S.A. ...37 F10
Khabarovsk, Russia ...19 E14
Kharkov, Ukraine ...18 E4
Khartoum = El Khartûm, Sudan ...27 E11
Khíos, Greece ...15 E11
Khulna, Bangladesh ...24 D6
Kidderminster, U.K. ...9 E5
Kiel, Ger. ...16 A5
Kielce, Poland ...17 C10
Kikládhes, Greece ...15 F11
Kikwit, Zaïre ...28 E3
Kildare, Ire. ...11 C5
Kilimanjaro, Tanzania ...28 E7
Kilkenny, Ire. ...11 D4
Killarney, Ire. ...11 D2
Kilmarnock, U.K. ...10 F4
Kimberley, Australia ...32 B4
Kimberley, S. Africa ...29 K4
King I., Australia ...33 F7
King William I., Canada ...34 B10
Kings Lynn, U.K. ...8 E8
Kingston, Jamaica ...38 J17
Kingston, U.K. ...9 F7
Kingussie, U.K. ...10 D4
Kinshasa, Zaïre ...28 E3
Kintyre, U.K. ...10 F3
Kiribati, Pac. Ocean ...3 D18
Kirkûk, Iraq ...25 B3
Kirkcaldy, U.K. ...10 E5
Kirkwall, U.K. ...10 C6
Kiruna, Swed. ...6 C15
Kisangani, Zaïre ...28 D5
Kishinev, Moldova ...18 D3
Kitakyūshū, Japan ...21 C2
Kitchener, Canada ...35 D11
Kíthira, Greece ...15 F10
Kitwe, Zambia ...29 G5
Kiva, L., Africa ...28 E5
Klyev, Ukraine ...18 D4
Klagenfurt, Austria ...16 E7
Knockmealdown Mts., Ire. ...11 D4
Knossos, Greece ...15 G11
Knoxville, U.S.A. ...37 C10
Kobe, Japan ...21 B4
København, Den. ...7 J12
Koblenz, Ger. ...16 C3
Kōchi, Japan ...21 C3
Kodiak I., Alaska ...34 C4
Kolding, Den. ...7 J10
Köln, Ger. ...16 C3
Komsomolsk, Russia ...19 D14
Kongsvinger, Norw. ...7 F12
Konya, Turkey ...25 B2
Kopervik, Norw. ...7 G8
Kopparberg, Swed. ...7 F12
Kōriyama, Japan ...21 G11
Kos, Greece ...15 F12
Košice, Slovak Rep. ...17 D10
Koskiusko, Mt., Australia ...33 F8
Kosovo, Asia ...15 C9
Kowloon, Hong Kong ...22 D6
Kraków, Poland ...17 C9
Krasnodar, Russia ...18 E4
Krasnoyarsk, Russia ...19 D10
Krefeld, Ger. ...16 C3
Kristiansand, Norw. ...7 G10
Kristianstad, Swed. ...7 J13
Kristiansund, Norw. ...6 E9
Kriti, Greece ...15 G11
Krivoy Rog, Ukraine ...18 E4
Kronoberg, Swed. ...7 H13
Kuala Lumpur, Malaysia ...23 C2
Kumamoto, Japan ...21 C2
Kumasi, Ghana ...26 G4
Kuopio, Fin. ...6 E19
Kurashiki, Japan ...21 B3
Kure, Japan ...21 B3
Kurilskiye Ostrova, Russia ...19 E16
Kushiro, Japan ...21 F11
Kuwait, Asia ...25 C3
Kuybyshev = Samara, Russia ...18 D6
Kwangju, S. Korea ...22 C7
Kyūshū, Japan ...21 C2
Kyle of Lochalsh, U.K. ...10 D3
Kyoga, L., Uganda ...28 D6
Kyōto, Japan ...21 B4
Kyrgyzstan, Asia ...18 E8
Kyyiv = Kiyev, Ukraine ...18 D4

L

La Boca, Panama ...38 H14
La Chorrera, Panama ...38 H14
La Coruña, Spain ...13 A1
La Habana, Cuba ...39 C8
La Paz, Bolivia ...40 G5
La Plata, Argentina ...42 D5
La Rioja, Spain ...13 A4
La Rochelle, France ...12 C3
La Spézia, Italy ...14 B3

Index

Labrador, Coast of, *Canada* 35 C13
Ladozhskoye, Ozero, *Russia* 18 C4
Lagos, *Port.* 13 D1
Lagos, *Nigeria* 26 G5
Lahore, *Pak.* 24 B3
Lahti, *Fin.* 7 F18
Lakshadweep Is., *India* 24 F3
Lancashire, □ *U.K.* 8 D5
Lancaster, *U.K.* 8 C5
Lancaster Sd., *Canada* 35 A11
Landskrona, *Swed.* 7 J12
Languedoc, □ *France* 12 E5
Lansing, *U.S.A.* 37 B10
Lanzhou, *China* 22 C5
Laois, □ *Ire.* 11 D4
Laos, ■ *Asia* 23 B2
Lapi, □ *Fin.* 6 C19
Lappland, *Fin.* 6 B18
Laptev Sea, *Arctic* 19 B13
Laredo, *U.S.A.* 36 E7
Lárisa, *Greece* 15 E10
Larne, □ *U.K.* 11 B6
Las Palmas, *Canary Is.* 26 C1
Las Vegas, *U.S.A.* 36 C3
Latvia, ■ *Europe* 18 D3
Lauchhammer, *Ger.* 16 C6
Launceston, *Australia* 33 G8
Lausanne, *Switz.* 16 E3
Lawton, *U.S.A.* 36 D7
Le Havre, *France* 12 B4
Le Mans, *France* 12 B4
Le Moule, *Guadeloupe* 38 L20
Leamington, *U.K.* 9 E6
Lebanon, ■ *Asia* 25 B2
Lecce, *Italy* 15 D8
Leeds, *U.K.* 8 D6
Leeuwarden, *Neth.* 16 B2
Leeward Is., *W. Indies* 39 D12
Legnica, *Poland* 16 C3
Leicester, *U.K.* 9 E6
Leicestershire, □ *U.K.* 9 E6
Leiden, *Neth.* 16 B2
Leinster, *Ire.* 11 C4
Leipzig, *Ger.* 16 C6
Leith, *U.K.* 10 F5
Leitrim, □ *Ire.* 11 B3
Lena, ≈ *Russia* 19 B13
Leningrad = St. Peterburg, *Russia* ..18 D4
León, *Mexico* 38 C4
León, *Spain* 13 A3
Lérida, *Spain* 13 B6
Lesotho, ■ *Africa* 29 K5
Lesser Antilles, *W. Indies* 39 E12
Lésvos, *Greece* 15 E11
Letchworth, *U.K.* 9 F7
Lethbridge, *Canada* 34 D8
Levkás, *Greece* 15 E9
Levkôsia, *Cyprus* 25 B2
Lewis, *U.K.* 10 C2
Lhasa, *China* 22 D4
Lianyungang, *China* 22 C6
Liberec, *Czech. Rep.* 16 C7
Liberia, ■ *Africa* 26 G3
Lībīya, Sahrâ', *Africa* 27 C9
Libreville, *Gabon* 28 D1
Libya, ■ *Africa* 27 C8
Liechtenstein, ■ *Europe* 16 E4
Liège, *Belgium* 16 C2
Liffey, ≈ *Ire.* 11 C5
Liguria, □ *Italy* 14 B3
Ligurian Sea, *Italy* 14 C3
Likasi, *Zaïre* 28 G5
Lille, *France* 12 A5
Lillehammer, *Norw.* 7 F11
Lilongwe, *Malawi* 29 G6
Lima, *Peru* 40 F3
Limavady, *U.K.* 11 A5
Limerick, *Ire.* 11 D3
Límnos, *Greece* 15 E11
Limoges, *France* 12 C4
Limousin, □ *France* 12 D4
Limpopo, ≈ *Africa* 29 K6
Linares, *Spain* 13 C4
Lincoln, *U.S.A.* 37 B7
Lincoln, *U.K.* 8 D7
Lincolnshire, □ *U.K.* 8 D7
Linköping, *Swed.* 7 G13
Linz, *Austria* 16 D7
Lisboa, *Port.* 13 C1
Lisburn, *U.K.* 11 B5
Listowel, *Ire.* 11 D2
Lithuania, ■ *Europe* 18 D3
Little Minch, *U.K.* 10 D2
Little Rock, *U.S.A.* 37 D8
Liverpool, *U.K.* 8 D5
Livingston, *U.K.* 10 F5
Livingstone, *Zambia* 29 H5
Livorno, *Italy* 14 C4
Lizard, *U.K.* 9 H2
Ljubljana, *Slovenia* 14 A6
Llanelli, *U.K.* 9 F3
Lloret, *Spain* 13 B7
Lobito, *Angola* 29 G2
Locarno, L. di, *Italy* 14 A3
Lochaber, *U.K.* 10 E3
Lockerbie, *U.K.* 10 F5
Łódź, *Poland* 17 C9
Lofoten, *Norw.* 6 B12

Logroño, *Spain* 13 A4
Loire, ≈ *France* 12 C2
Lolland, *Den.* 7 J11
Lombardia, □ *Italy* 14 B3
Lombok, *Indonesia* 23 D3
Lomé, *Togo* 26 G5
Lomond, L., *U.K.* 10 E4
Łomza, *Poland* 17 B10
London, *U.K.* 9 F7
London, *Canada* 35 D11
Londonderry, *U.K.* 11 B4
Londrina, *Brazil* 42 A6
Long Beach, *U.S.A.* 36 D3
Long Island, *U.S.A.* 37 B12
Longford, □ *Ire.* 11 C4
Lorca, *Spain* 13 D5
Lorne, *U.K.* 10 E3
Lorraine, □ *France* 12 B7
Los Angeles, *U.S.A.* 36 D3
Lothian, □ *U.K.* 10 F5
Loughborough, *U.K.* 8 E6
Louisiana, □ *U.S.A.* 37 D8
Louisville, *U.S.A.* 37 C9
Lourdes, *France* 12 E3
Louth, □ *Ire.* 11 C5
Lower Hutt, *N.Z.* 31 J5
Lowestoft, *U.K.* 9 E9
Luanda, *Angola* 28 F2
Luanshya, *Zambia* 29 G5
Lubbock, *U.S.A.* 36 D6
Lübeck, *Ger.* 16 B5
Lublin, *Poland* 17 C11
Lubumbashi, *Zaïre* 29 G5
Lucca, *Italy* 14 C4
Lucknow, *India* 24 C4
Ludwigshafen, *Ger.* 16 D4
Lugo, *Spain* 13 A2
Luleå, *Swed.* 6 D17
Lüneburger Heide, *Ger.* 16 B5
Lurgan, *U.K.* 11 B5
Lusaka, *Zambia* 29 H5
Luton, *U.K.* 9 F7
Luxembourg, ■ *Europe* 16 D3
Luzern, *Switz.* 16 E4
Luzhou, *China* 22 D5
Luzon, *Philippines* 23 B4
Lvov, *Ukraine* 18 E3
Lyckseke, *Swed.* 6 D15
Lymington, *U.K.* 9 G6
Lyon, *France* 12 D6

M

M'Clintock Chan., *Canada* 34 B9
Macapá, *Brazil* 41 C8
Macau, *Asia* 22 D6
Macclesfield, *U.K.* 8 D5
Macdonnell Ranges, *Australia* 32 C5
Macedonia, ■ *Europe* 15 D9
Maceió, *Brazil* 41 E11
Mackenzie, ≈ *Canada* 34 B6
Mackenzie Mts., *Canada* 34 B6
Macroom, *Ire.* 11 E3
Madagascar, ■ *Africa* 29 J9
Madeira, *Atl. Ocean* 26 B1
Madeira, ≈ *S. Amer.* 40 E6
Madhya Pradesh, □ *India* 24 D4
Madison, *U.S.A.* 37 B9
Madras, *India* 24 F5
Madre, L., *Mexico* 38 B5
Madrid, *Spain* 13 B4
Madrid, *Spain* 13 B4
Madurai, *India* 24 G4
Maebashi, *Japan* 21 A6
Mafia I., *Tanzania* 28 F7
Magadan, *Russia* 19 D16
Magalluf, *Spain* 13 C7
Magdeburg, *Ger.* 16 B6
Magherafelt, □ *U.K.* 11 B5
Maharashtra, □ *India* 24 D4
Mahon, *Spain* 13 C8
Mai-Ndombe, L., *Zaïre* 28 E3
Maidenhead, *U.K.* 9 F7
Maidstone, *U.K.* 9 F8
Maiduguri, *Nigeria* 27 F7
Maimana, *Afghan.* 25 B5
Maine, □ *France* 12 B3
Maine, □ *U.S.A.* 37 A13
Mainz, *Ger.* 16 D4
Makasar = Ujung Pandang,
   Indonesia 23 D3
Makedhona, □ *Greece* 15 D10
Makgadikgadi Salt Pans, *Botswana* ...29 J5
Makkah, *S. Arabia* 25 C3
Malaga, *Spain* 13 D3
Malatya, *Turkey* 25 B2
Malawi, ■ *Africa* 29 G6
Malaysia, ■ *Asia* 23 C2
Maldives, ■ *Ind. Ocean* 24 G3
Mali, ■ *Africa* 26 E4
Mallorca, *Spain* 13 C7
Mallow, *Ire.* 11 D3
Malmö, *Swed.* 7 J12
Malmöhus, □ *Swed.* 7 J12
Malta, ■ *Europe* 14 G6
Malvern Hills, *U.K.* 9 E5
Man, I. of, *U.K.* 8 C3
Managua, *Nicaragua* 38 E7

Manaus, *Brazil* 40 D6
Manchester, *U.K.* 8 D5
Mandalay, *Burma* 24 D8
Manila, *Philippines* 23 B4
Manitoba, □ *Canada* 34 C10
Manitoba, L., *Canada* 34 C10
Manizales, *Colombia* 40 B3
Mannheim, *Ger.* 16 D4
Mansel I., *Canada* 35 B11
Mansfield, *U.K.* 8 D6
Mantova, *Italy* 14 B4
Maputo, *Mozambique* 29 K6
Mar del Plata, *Argentina* 42 D5
Maracaibo, *Venezuela* 40 A4
Maracay, *Venezuela* 40 A5
Marajó, I. de, *Brazil* 41 D9
Maranhão, □ *Brazil* 41 E9
Marbella, *Spain* 13 D3
Marche, □ *France* 12 C4
Marche, □ *Italy* 14 C5
Margate, *U.K.* 9 F9
Mariana Is., *Pac. Ocean* 3 D17
Maribor, *Slovenia* 14 A6
Marie-Galante, *W. Indies* 38 M20
Marília, *Brazil* 41 H8
Maringá, *Brazil* 42 A6
Marmara, Sea of, *Turkey* 25 A1
Marquesas Is., *Pac. Ocean* 2 E3
Marrakech, *Morocco* 26 B3
Marseille, *France* 12 E6
Marshall Is., ■ *Pac. Ocean* 3 D18
Martha's Vineyard, *U.S.A.* 37 B12
Martinique, □ *W. Indies* 38 N21
Maryland, □ *U.S.A.* 37 C11
Mashhad, *Iran* 25 B4
Masqat, *Oman* 25 C4
Massachusetts, □ *U.S.A.* 37 B12
Massif Central, *France* 12 D5
Matadi, *Zaïre* 28 F2
Matamoros, *Mexico* 38 B5
Mato Grosso, □ *Brazil* 41 F7
Mato Grosso do Sul, □ *Brazil* 41 G7
Matsuyama, *Japan* 21 C3
Matterhorn, *Switz.* 16 E3
Maturín, *Venezuela* 40 B6
Mauritania, ■ *Africa* 26 E2
Mauritius, ■ *Ind. Ocean* 30 H9
Mayo, □ *Ire.* 11 C2
Mazar-i-Sharif, *Afghan.* 25 B5
Mbandaka, *Zaïre* 28 D3
Meath, □ *Ire.* 11 C5
Mecca = Makkah, *S. Arabia* 25 C2
Mechelen, *Belgium* 16 C2
Medan, *Indonesia* 23 C1
Medellín, *Colombia* 40 B3
Medicine Hat, *Canada* 34 D8
Medina = Al Madinah, *S. Arabia* 25 C2
Mediterranean Sea, ...5 H7
Meerut, *India* 24 C4
Meknès, *Morocco* 26 B3
Mekong, ≈ *Asia* 23 B2
Melbourne, *Australia* 33 F8
Melrose, *U.K.* 10 F6
Melville Is., *Australia* 32 A5
Memphis, *U.S.A.* 37 C9
Menai Strait, *U.K.* 8 D3
Mendip Hills, *U.K.* 9 F5
Mendoza, *Argentina* 42 C3
Menorca, *Spain* 13 B8
Mentawai Is., *Indonesia* 23 D1
Merca, *Somalia* 30 F8
Mérida, *Mexico* 38 C7
Mersey, ≈ *U.K.* 8 D5
Merseyside, □ *U.K.* 8 D4
Merthyr Tydfil, *U.K.* 9 F4
Messina, *Italy* 14 E6
Metz, *France* 12 B7
Mexicali, *Mexico* 38 A1
Mexico, ■ *Cent. Amer.* 38 B3
Mexico City, *Mexico* 38 D5
Mexico, G. de, *Cent. Amer.* 38 B6
Miami, *U.S.A.* 37 E10
Michigan, □ *U.S.A.* 37 A9
Michigan, L., *U.S.A.* 37 B9
Micronesia, ■ *Pac. Ocean* 3 D17
Mid Glamorgan, □ *U.K.* 9 F4
Middlesbrough, *U.K.* 8 C6
Midland, *U.S.A.* 36 D6
Mikkeli, □ *Fin.* 6 E19
Milano, *Italy* 14 B3
Milton Keynes, *U.K.* 9 E7
Milwaukee, *U.S.A.* 37 B9
Minas Gerais, □ *Brazil* 41 G9
Mindanao, *Philippines* 23 C4
Minneapolis, *U.S.A.* 37 B8
Minnesota, □ *U.S.A.* 37 A8
Minsk, *Belarus* 18 D4
Miskolc, *Hungary* 17 D10
Misrâtah, *Libya* 27 B8
Mississippi, □ *U.S.A.* 37 D9
Mississippi, ≈ *U.S.A.* 37 E9
Missouri, □ *U.S.A.* 37 C8
Missouri, ≈ *U.S.A.* 37 C8
Miyako, *Japan* 21 G11
Mobile, *U.S.A.* 37 D9
Mobutu, L., *Africa* 28 D6
Moçambique, *Mozambique* 29 H8
Módena, *Italy* 14 B4
Mogadishu, *Somalia* 30 E8

Moldova, ■ *Europe* 18 E3
Molise, □ *Italy* 14 D6
Mölndal, *Swed.* 7 H12
Moluccas, *Indonesia* 23 C4
Mombasa, *Kenya* 28 E7
Mona, Canal de la, *W. Indies* 39 D11
Monaco, ■ *Europe* 12 E7
Monaghan, □ *Ire.* 11 B5
Mönchengladbach, *Ger.* 16 C3
Moncton, *Canada* 35 D13
Mongolia, ■ *Asia* 22 B5
Monrovia, *Liberia* 26 G2
Mont St.-Michel, *France* 12 B3
Montana, □ *U.S.A.* 36 A4
Monte Carlo, *Monaco* 12 E7
Montego Bay, *Jamaica* 38 J16
Montenegro, □ *Yug.* 15 C8
Monterrey, *Mexico* 38 B4
Montes Claros, *Brazil* 41 G10
Montevideo, *Uruguay* 42 C5
Montgomery, *U.S.A.* 37 D9
Montpellier, *France* 12 E5
Montréal, *Canada* 35 D12
Montrose, *U.K.* 10 E6
Montserrat, *W. Indies* 38 L19
Moray Firth, *U.K.* 10 D5
More og Romsdal, □ *Norw.* 6 E9
Morecambe B., *U.K.* 8 C4
Morelia, *Mexico* 38 D4
Morena, Sierra, *Spain* 13 C3
Morioka, *Japan* 21 G11
Morocco, ■ *Africa* 26 B3
Morvern, *U.K.* 10 E3
Moscow = Moskva, *Russia* 18 D4
Mosel, ≈ *Ger.* 16 C3
Moskva, *Russia* 18 D4
Mostaganem, *Algeria* 26 A5
Motala, *Swed.* 7 G13
Motherwell, *U.K.* 10 F5
Moulamyaing, *Burma* 24 E8
Mourne Mts., *U.K.* 11 B5
Mozambique, ■ *Africa* 29 H6
Mozambique Chan., *Africa* 29 H8
Muck, *U.K.* 10 E2
Mufulira, *Zambia* 29 G5
Mülheim, *Ger.* 16 C3
Mulhouse, *France* 12 C7
Mull, *U.K.* 10 E3
Mullet Pen., *Ire.* 11 B1
Mullingar, *Ire.* 11 C4
Multan, *Pak.* 24 B3
München, *Ger.* 16 D5
Munich = München, *Ger.* 16 D5
Munster, *Ire.* 11 D3
Münster, *Ger.* 16 B3
Murcia, □ *Spain* 13 C5
Murcia, *Spain* 13 C5
Murmansk, *Russia* 18 C4
Muroran, *Japan* 21 F11
Murray River, ≈ *Australia* 33 F6
Murray River Basin, *Australia* 33 E7
Musgrave Ranges, *Australia* 32 D5
Mustique, *W. Indies* 38 Q20
Mwanza, *Tanzania* 28 E6
Myanmar = Burma, ■ *Asia* 24 D8
Mysore, *India* 24 F4

N

Nagano, *Japan* 21 A6
Nagaoka, *Japan* 21 G10
Nagasaki, *Japan* 21 C1
Nagoya, *Japan* 21 B5
Nagpur, *India* 24 D4
Nairobi, *Kenya* 28 E7
Nakhodka, *Russia* 19 E14
Namaland, *Namibia* 29 J3
Namibia, ■ *Africa* 29 J3
Namibwoestyn, *Namibia* 29 J2
Namsos, *Norw.* 6 D11
Nanchang, *China* 22 D6
Nancy, *France* 12 B7
Nanjing, *China* 22 C6
Nanning, *China* 22 D5
Nansei-Shoto, *Japan* 21 J8
Nantes, *France* 12 C3
Napier, *N.Z.* 31 H6
Napoli, *Italy* 14 D6
Narbonne, *France* 12 E5
Narvik, *Norw.* 6 B14
Naser, Buheiret en, *Egypt* 27 D11
Nashville, *U.S.A.* 37 C9
Nassau, *Bahamas* 39 B9
Natal, *Brazil* 41 E11
Nauru, ■ *Pac. Ocean* 3 E12
Navarra, □ *Spain* 13 A5
Náxos, *Greece* 15 F11
Ndjamena, *Chad* 27 F8
Ndola, *Zambia* 29 G5
Nebraska, □ *U.S.A.* 36 B6
Negro, ≈ *Brazil* 40 D6
Neiva, *Colombia* 40 C3
Nemuro, *Japan* 21 F12
Nemuro-Kaikyō, *Japan* 21 F12
Nenagh, *Ire.* 11 D3
Nepal, ■ *Asia* 24 C5
Ness, L., *U.K.* 10 D4
Netherlands, ■ *Europe* 16 B2
Nevada, □ *U.S.A.* 36 C3

Nevers, *France* 12 C5
New Bedford, *U.S.A.* 37 B12
New Britain, *Pac. Ocean* 3 E17
New Brunswick, □ *Canada* 35 D13
New Caledonia, *Pac. Ocean* 3 F18
New Forest, *U.K.* 9 G6
New Hampshire, □ *U.S.A.* 37 B12
New Haven, *U.S.A.* 37 B12
New Jersey, □ *U.S.A.* 37 C12
New Mexico, □ *U.S.A.* 36 D5
New Orleans, *U.S.A.* 37 E9
New Plymouth, *N.Z.* 31 H5
New Providence I., *W. Indies* 39 B9
New South Wales, □ *Australia* 33 E8
New York, *U.S.A.* 37 B12
New York, □ *U.S.A.* 37 B11
New Zealand, ■ *Pac. Ocean* 31 J5
Newark, *U.S.A.* 37 B12
Newbury, *U.K.* 9 F6
Newcastle, *Australia* 33 E9
Newcastle, *U.K.* 8 C6
Newcastle-under-Lyme, *U.K.* 8 D5
Newfoundland, □ *Canada* 35 C14
Newport, *U.K.* 9 F5
Newport News, *U.S.A.* 37 C11
Newquay, *U.K.* 9 G2
Newry, *U.K.* 11 B5
Newtonabbey, □ *U.K.* 11 B6
Newtownards, *U.K.* 11 B6
Niagara Falls, *N. Amer.* 35 D12
Niamey, *Niger* 26 F5
Nicaragua, ■ *Cent. Amer.* 38 E7
Nice, *France* 12 E7
Nicobar Is., *India* 24 G7
Niederösterreich, □ *Austria* 16 D7
Niedersachsen, □ *Ger.* 16 B4
Niger, ■ *Africa* 26 E6
Niger, ≈ *Africa* 26 G6
Nigeria, ■ *Africa* 26 G6
Niigata, *Japan* 21 G10
Nijmegen, *Neth.* 16 C2
Nîl el Abyad, ≈ *Africa* 27 E11
Nîl el Azraq, ≈ *Africa* 27 E11
Nîl, Nahr en, ≈ *Africa* 27 C11
Nile = Nîl, Nahr en, ≈ *Africa* 27 C11
Nîmes, *France* 12 E6
Ningbo, *China* 22 D7
Nishinomiya, *Japan* 21 B4
Niteroi, *Brazil* 41 H10
Nizhniy Novgorod, *Russia* 18 D5
Nord-Trondelag, □ *Norw.* 6 E10
Nordland, □ *Norw.* 6 C13
Nordrhein-Westfalen, □ *Ger.* 16 C3
Norfolk, *U.S.A.* 37 C11
Norfolk, □ *U.K.* 8 E8
Normandie, □ *France* 12 B3
Norrbotten, □ *Norw.* 6 C15
Norrköping, *Swed.* 7 G14
North Carolina, □ *U.S.A.* 37 C11
North Channel, *Europe* 8 C2
North Dakota, □ *U.S.A.* 36 A6
North Downs, *U.K.* 9 F7
North Island, *N.Z.* 31 G5
North Korea, ■ *Asia* 22 B7
North Minch, *U.K.* 10 C3
North Ronaldsay, *U.K.* 10 B6
North Sea, *Europe* 8 C8
North Uist, *U.K.* 10 D1
North West Highlands, *U.K.* 10 D3
North West Territories, □ *Canada* ...34 B8
North Yorkshire, □ *U.K.* 8 C6
North Yorkshire Moors, *U.K.* 8 C7
Northampton, *U.K.* 9 E7
Northamptonshire, □ *U.K.* 9 E7
Northern Ireland, □ *U.K.* 11 B4
Northern Territory, □ *Australia* 32 B5
Northumberland, □ *U.K.* 8 B5
Norway, ■ *Europe* 6 E11
Norwegian Sea, *Atl. Ocean* 4 D9
Norwich, *U.K.* 8 E9
Nottingham, *U.K.* 8 E6
Nottinghamshire, □ *U.K.* 8 D6
Nouakchott, *Mauritania* 26 E1
Nova Scotia, □ *Canada* 35 D13
Novaya Zemlya, *Russia* 18 B6
Novi Sad, *Serbia* 15 B8
Novokuznetsk, *Russia* 18 D9
Novosibirsk, *Russia* 18 D9
Novosibirskiye Ostrova, *Russia* 19 B15
Nûbîya, Es Sahrâ en, *Sudan* 27 D11
Nullarbor Plain, *Australia* 32 E4
Nuneaton, *U.K.* 9 E6
Nunivak I., *Alaska* 34 B3
Nürnberg, *Ger.* 16 D5
Nyasa, L., *Africa* 29 G6
Nykøbing, *Den.* 7 J12

O

Oakland, *U.S.A.* 36 C2
Ob, ≈ *Russia* 18 C7
Oban, *U.K.* 10 E3
Oberhausen, *Ger.* 16 C3
Oberösterreich, □ *Austria* 16 D6
Obihiro, *Japan* 21 F11
Odense, *Den.* 7 J11
Oder, ≈ *Europe* 16 B7
Odessa, *Ukraine* 18 E4
Odessa, *U.S.A.* 36 D6

ffaly, □ Ire. ...11 C4
ffenbach, Ger. ...16 C4
gbomosho, Nigeria ...26 G5
gden, U.S.A. ...36 B4
hio, ≈ U.S.A. ...37 C9
hio, □ U.S.A. ...37 B10
kavango Swamps, Botswana ...29 H4
kayama, Japan ...21 B3
kazaki, Japan ...21 B5
khotsk, Russia ...19 D15
khotsk Sea of, Arctic ...19 D15
ki-Shotō, Japan ...21 A3
klahoma, □ U.S.A. ...37 C7
klahoma City, U.S.A. ...37 C7
land, Swed. ...7 H14
ldenburg, Ger. ...16 B4
ldham, U.K. ...8 D5
limbos, Greece ...15 D10
lomouc, Czech Rep. ...16 D8
lympia, Greece ...15 F9
magh, U.K. ...11 B4
maha, U.S.A. ...37 B7
man, ■ Asia ...25 C4
man, Gulf of, Asia ...25 C4
mdurmân, Sudan ...27 E11
msk, Russia ...18 D8
muta, Japan ...21 C2
nezhskoye, Ozero, Russia ...18 D4
nitsha, Nigeria ...26 G6
ntario, □ Canada ...35 C11
ntario, L., N. Amer. ...35 D12
pava, Czech Rep. ...17 D8
ppland, □ Norw. ...7 H14
radea, Rom. ...17 E10
ran, Algeria ...26 A4
ranje, ≈ S. Africa ...29 K3
rebro, □ Swed. ...7 G13
regon, □ U.S.A. ...36 B2
rense, Spain ...13 A2
rinoco, ≈ S. Amer. ...40 B6
rissa, □ India ...24 D5
rkney, □ U.K. ...10 D5
rlando, U.S.A. ...37 E10
rléanais, □ France ...12 C4
rléans, France ...12 C4
rumiyeh, Iran ...25 B3
ruro, Bolivia ...40 G5
saka, Japan ...21 B4
shawa, Canada ...35 D12
shogbo, Nigeria ...26 G5
sijek, Croatia ...15 B8
ckarshamn, Swed. ...7 H14
slo, Norw. ...7 G11
snabrück, Ger. ...16 B4
stersund, Swed. ...6 E13
stfriesische Inseln, Ger. ...16 B3
strava, Czech Rep. ...17 D9
strov Vrangelya, Russia ...19 B18
sumi-Kaikyō, Japan ...21 D2
sumi-Shotō, Japan ...21 D2
tanu, Japan ...21 F11
tranto, Str. of, Italy ...15 D8
ttawa, Canada ...35 D12
tztal, Austria ...16 E5
uagadougou, Burkina Faso ...26 F4
ujda, Morocco ...26 B4
ulu, Fin. ...6 D18
uter Hebrides, U.K. ...10 D1
viedo, Spain ...13 A3
wambo, Namibia ...29 H3
x Mts., Ire. ...11 B3
xford, U.K. ...9 F6
xfordshire, □ U.K. ...9 F6

acaraima, Sierra, S. Amer. ...40 C6
acific Ocean, ...2 D3
adang, Indonesia ...23 D2
adova, Italy ...14 B4
aisley, U.K. ...10 F4
akistan, ■ Asia ...24 C2
alawan, Philippines ...23 B3
alembang, Indonesia ...23 D2
alencia, Spain ...13 A3
alermo, Italy ...14 E5
alma, Spain ...13 C7
almerston North, N.Z. ...31 J5
almira, Colombia ...40 C3
amplona, Spain ...13 A5
anama, ■ Cent. Amer. ...39 F8
anama Canal, Panama ...38 H14
anama, G. de, Panama ...39 H14
apua New Guinea, ■ Pac. Ocean ...3 H12
ará, □ Brazil ...41 D8
araguay, ■ S. Amer. ...42 A5
araíba, □ Brazil ...41 E11
aramaribo, Surinam ...41 B7
arana, ≈ S. Amer. ...42 C5
araná, □ Brazil ...42 A6
araná, Argentina ...42 C4
arecis, Serra dos, Brazil ...40 F6
aris, France ...12 B5
arma, Italy ...14 B4
asadena, U.S.A. ...36 D4
asto, Colombia ...40 C3
atna, India ...24 C6

Patos L. dos, Brazil ...42 C6
Patrai, Greece ...15 E9
Pavia, Italy ...14 B3
Pecs, Hungary ...17 E9
Peking = Beijing, China ...22 C6
Pelopónnisos, □ Greece ...15 F10
Pelotas, Brazil ...42 C6
Pemba I., Tanzania ...28 F7
Pennine Range, U.K. ...8 C5
Pennsylvania, □ U.S.A. ...37 B11
Penzance, U.K. ...9 G2
Peoria, U.S.A. ...37 B9
Pereira, Colombia ...40 C3
Perm, Russia ...18 D6
Pernambuco, □ Brazil ...41 E11
Perpignan, France ...12 E5
Perth, Australia ...32 E2
Perth, U.K. ...10 E5
Peru, ■ S. Amer. ...40 E3
Perúgia, Italy ...14 C5
Pésaro, Italy ...14 C5
Pescara, Italy ...14 C6
Peshawar, Pak. ...24 B3
Potorboro', Canada ...35 D12
Peterborough, U.K. ...9 E7
Peterhead, U.K. ...10 D7
Petropavlovsk-Kamchatskiy, Russia ...19 D16
Petrópolis, Brazil ...41 H10
Pforzheim, Ger. ...16 D4
Phan Bho Ho Chi Minh, Vietnam ...23 B2
Philadelphia, U.S.A. ...37 B12
Philippi, Greece ...15 D11
Philippines, ■ Asia ...23 B4
Phnom Penh, Cambodia ...23 B2
Phoenix, U.S.A. ...36 D4
Phoenix Is., Pac. Ocean ...2 E1
Piacenza, Italy ...14 B3
Piauí, □ Brazil ...41 E10
Picardie, □ France ...12 A5
Piemonte, □ Italy ...14 B2
Pietermaritzburg, S. Africa ...29 K6
Pindos Oros, Greece ...15 C9
Piotrków Trybunalsk, Poland ...17 C9
Piracicaba, Brazil ...41 H9
Piraievs, Greece ...15 F10
Pisa, Italy ...14 C4
Pistóia, Italy ...14 C4
Piteå, Swed. ...6 D16
Pittsburgh, U.S.A. ...37 B11
Plauen, Ger. ...16 C6
Pleven, Bulg. ...15 C11
Ploiești, Rom. ...17 F12
Plovdiv, Bulg. ...15 C11
Plymouth, U.K. ...9 G3
Plzeň, Czech Rep. ...16 D6
Po, ≈ Italy ...14 B5
Podgorica, Yug. ...15 C8
Pointe Noire, Congo ...28 E2
Pointe-à-Pitre, Guadeloupe ...38 L20
Poitou, □ France ...12 C3
Poland, ■ Europe ...17 C9
Ponce, Puerto Rico ...39 D11
Pondicherry, India ...24 F4
Ponta Grossa, Brazil ...42 B6
Pontefract, U.K. ...8 D6
Pontevedra, Spain ...13 A1
Pontiac, U.S.A. ...37 B10
Pontypool, U.K. ...9 F4
Pontypridd, U.K. ...9 F4
Poole, U.K. ...9 G6
Poona = Pune, India ...24 E3
Poopó, L., Bolivia ...40 G5
Popocatepetl, Mexico ...38 D5
Pori, Fin. ...7 F16
Port au Prince, Haiti ...39 D10
Port Elizabeth, S. Africa ...29 L5
Port Glasgow, U.K. ...10 F4
Port Harcourt, Nigeria ...26 H6
Port Laoise, Ire. ...11 C3
Port of Spain, Trinidad ...38 S20
Port Said = Bûr Saîd, Egypt ...27 B11
Port Talbot, U.K. ...9 F4
Portland, U.S.A. ...36 A2
Porto, Port. ...13 B1
Pôrto Alegre, Brazil ...42 C6
Portree, U.K. ...10 D2
Portsmouth, U.K. ...9 G6
Portsmouth, U.S.A. ...37 C11
Portugal, ■ Europe ...13 C1
Potosí, Bolivia ...40 G5
Potsdam, Ger. ...16 B6
Powys, □ U.K. ...9 E4
Poznan, Poland ...16 B8
Prague = Praha, Czech Rep. ...16 C7
Praha, Czech Rep. ...16 C7
Prato, Italy ...14 C4
Preston, U.K. ...8 D5
Pretoria, S. Africa ...29 K5
Prince Albert, Canada ...34 C9
Prince Charles I., Canada ...35 B12
Prince Edward I., □ Canada ...35 D13
Prince of Wales I., Alaska ...34 C6
Prince of Wales I., Canada ...34 A10
Provence, □ France ...12 E6
Providence, U.S.A. ...37 B12
Puebla, Mexico ...38 D5
Pueblo, U.S.A. ...36 C6
Puerto Rico, ■ W. Indies ...39 D11

Puglia, □ Italy ...14 D7
Pula, Croatia ...14 B5
Pune, India ...24 E3
Punjab, □ India ...24 B4
Purbeck, I. of, U.K. ...9 G5
Pusan, S. Korea ...22 C7
Pyongyang, N. Korea ...22 C7
Pyrenées, France ...12 E4

Q
Qatar, ■ Asia ...25 C4
Qingdao, China ...22 C7
Qiqihar, China ...22 B7
Quantock Hills, U.K. ...9 F4
Quebec, □ Canada ...35 C13
Quebec, Canada ...35 D12
Queen Charlotte Is., Canada ...34 C6
Queen Maud Gulf, Canada ...34 B9
Queensland, □ Australia ...33 C7
Quezon City, Philippines ...23 B4
Quito, Ecuador, ...40 D3

R
Rabat, Morocco ...26 B3
Radom, Poland ...17 C10
Ragusa, Italy ...14 F6
Rajasthan, □ India ...24 C3
Ramsgate, U.K. ...9 F9
Randers, Den. ...7 H11
Rangoon, Burma ...24 E8
Rasht, Iran ...25 B3
Rathlin I., U.K. ...11 A5
Rauma, Fin. ...7 F16
Ravenna, Italy ...14 B5
Rawalpindi, Pak. ...24 B3
Reading, U.K. ...9 F7
Rebun-Tō, Japan ...21 E11
Recife, Brazil ...41 E12
Red River, ≈ U.S.A. ...37 D8
Red Sea, Asia ...25 C2
Redditch, U.K. ...9 E6
Regensburg, Ger. ...16 D6
Réggio di Calábria, Italy ...14 E6
Réggio nell'Emilia, Italy ...14 B4
Regina, Canada ...34 C9
Reichenbach, Ger. ...16 C6
Reigate, U.K. ...9 F7
Reims, France ...12 B6
Reina Adelaida, Arch., Chile ...42 G2
Reindeer L., Canada ...34 C9
Remscheid, Ger. ...16 C3
Rennes, France ...12 B3
Reno, U.S.A. ...36 C3
Réunion, ■ Ind. Ocean ...30 H9
Rhein, ≈ Europe ...16 C3
Rheinland Pfalz, □ Ger. ...16 D3
Rhine = Rhein, ≈ Ger. ...16 C3
Rhode Island, □ U.S.A. ...37 B12
Rhodes = Ródhos, Greece ...15 F13
Rhodopi Planina, Bulg. ...15 D11
Rhön, Ger. ...16 C5
Rhondda, U.K. ...9 F4
Rhône, ≈ France ...12 D6
Rhum, I. of, U.K. ...10 E2
Ribeirão Prêto, Brazil ...41 H9
Richmond, U.K. ...9 F7
Richmond, U.S.A. ...37 C11
Riga, Latvia ...18 D3
Rijeka, Croatia ...14 B6
Rimini, Italy ...14 B5
Rio Branco, Brazil ...40 E5
Rio de Janeiro, Brazil ...41 H10
Rio Gallegos, Argentina ...42 G3
Rio Grande, Brazil ...42 C6
Rio Grande do Norte, □ Brazil ...41 E11
Rio Grande do Sul, □ Brazil ...42 B6
Riyadh = Ar Riyâd, S. Arabia ...25 C3
Rochefort, France ...12 D3
Rochester, U.K. ...9 F8
Rochester, U.S.A. ...37 B11
Rocky Mts., N. Amer. ...36 A4
Ródhos, Greece ...15 F13
Rogaland, □ Norw. ...7 G9
Roma, Italy ...14 D5
Romania, ■ Europe ...17 F12
Rondônia, □ Brazil ...40 F6
Roodepoort-Maraisburg, S. Africa ...29 K5
Roraima, □ Brazil ...40 C6
Rosario, Argentina ...42 C4
Roscommon, □ Ire. ...11 C3
Roseau, Dominica ...38 M20
Roskilde, Den. ...7 J12
Rostock, Ger. ...16 A6
Rostov, Russia ...18 E4
Rotherham, U.K. ...8 D6
Rotterdam, Neth. ...16 C2
Roubaix, Belgium ...16 C1
Rouen, France ...12 B4
Rousay, U.K. ...10 B5
Ruse, Bulg. ...15 C12
Russia, ■ Europe/Asia ...18 C7
Rwanda, ■ Africa ...28 E5
Ryde, U.K. ...9 G6

S
's-Gravenhage, Neth. ...16 B2
's-Hertogenbosch, Neth. ...16 C2
Saarbrucken, Ger. ...16 D3
Saarland, □ Ger. ...16 D3
Sabadell, Spain ...13 B6
Sabah, □ Malaysia ...23 C5
Sacramento, U.S.A. ...36 C2
Sado, Japan ...21 G10
Safi, Morocco ...26 B3
Saginaw, U.S.A. ...37 B10
Sahara, Africa ...26 D4
Saigon = Phanh Bho Ho Chi Minh, Vietnam ...23 B2
Saint John, Canada ...35 D13
Saintonge, □ France ...12 D3
Sakai, Japan ...21 B4
Sakata, Japan ...21 G10
Sakhalin, Russia ...19 D15
Salamanca, Spain ...13 B3
Salerno, Italy ...14 D6
Salford, U.K. ...8 D5
Salisbury, U.K. ...9 F6
Salt Lake City, U.S.A. ...36 B4
Salta, Argentina ...42 A3
Saltillo, Mexico ...38 B4
Salvador, Brazil ...41 F11
Salzburg, Austria ...16 E6
Salzgitter, Ger. ...16 B5
Samara, Russia ...18 D6
Samarkand, Uzbekistan ...18 F7
Samoan Is., Pac. Ocean ...31 A12
Sámos, Greece ...15 F12
Samothráki, Greece ...15 D11
San Angelo, U.S.A. ...36 D6
San Antonio, U.S.A. ...36 E7
San Cristóbal, Venezuela ...40 B4
San Diego, U.S.A. ...36 D3
San Fernando, Trinidad ...38 S20
San Francisco, U.S.A. ...36 C2
San Francisco de Macorís, Dom. Rep. ...39 D10
San Jose, U.S.A. ...36 C2
San Juan, Argentina ...42 C3
San Juan, Puerto Rico ...39 D11
San Luis Potosí, Mexico ...38 C4
San Marino, ■ Europe ...14 C5
San Miguel de Tucuman, Argentina ...42 B3
San Salvador, El Salvador ...38 E7
San Sebastian, Spain ...13 A4
San'a, Yemen ...25 D3
Sancti Spíritus, Cuba ...39 C9
Sanday, U.K. ...10 B6
Santa Ana, U.S.A. ...36 D3
Santa Barbara, U.S.A. ...36 D3
Santa Catarina, □ Brazil ...42 B7
Santa Clara, Cuba ...39 C9
Santa Clara, U.S.A. ...36 C2
Santa Cruz, Bolivia ...40 G6
Santa Cruz, Canary Is. ...26 C1
Santa Fe, Argentina ...42 C4
Santa Marta, Colombia ...40 A4
Santander, Spain ...13 A4
Santarém, Brazil ...41 D8
Santarém, Port. ...13 C1
Santiago, Chile ...42 C2
Santiago, Dom. Rep. ...39 D10
Santiago, Spain ...13 A1
Santiago de Cuba, Cuba ...39 C9
Santo Domingo, Dom. Rep. ...39 D11
Santos, Brazil ...42 A7
São Francisco, ≈ Brazil ...41 F11
São Luís, Brazil ...41 D10
São Paulo, □ Brazil ...41 H9
São Paulo, Brazil ...42 A7
São Tomé & Principe, ■ Africa ...30 E4
Sapporo, Japan ...21 F11
Sarajevo, Bosnia ...15 C8
Saratov, Russia ...18 D5
Sarawak, □ Malaysia ...23 C4
Sardegna, □ Italy ...14 D3
Sardinia = Sardegna, □ Italy ...14 D3
Sark, Channel Is. ...12 B2
Sasebo, Japan ...21 C1
Saskatchewan, □ Canada ...34 C9
Saskatoon, Canada ...34 C9
Satu Mare, Rom. ...17 E11
Saudi Arabia, ■ Asia ...25 C3
Sault Ste. Marie, Canada ...35 D11
Savannah, U.S.A. ...37 D10
Savoie, □ France ...12 D7
Savona, Italy ...14 B3
Scapa Flow, U.K. ...10 C5
Scarborough, U.K. ...8 C7
Schleswig - Holstein, □ Ger. ...16 A4
Schwäbische Alb, Ger. ...16 D4
Schwarzwald, Ger. ...16 D4
Schwerin, Ger. ...16 B5
Scilly, Is. of, U.K. ...9 H2
Scotland, □ U.K. ...10 E4
Scunthorpe, U.K. ...8 D7
Seattle, U.S.A. ...36 A2
Segovia, Spain ...13 B3
Seine, ≈ France ...12 B4
Sekondi - Takoradi, Ghana ...26 H4
Selkirk, U.K. ...10 F6
Semarang, Indonesia ...23 D3
Sendai, Japan ...21 G11

Senegal, ■ Africa ...26 F2
Serbia, □ Yug. ...15 C9
Setonaikai, Japan ...21 C3
Setúbal, Port. ...13 C1
Sevastopol, Ukraine ...18 F4
Severn, ≈ U.K. ...9 F5
Severnaya Zemlya, Russia ...19 B10
Sevilla, Spain ...13 D3
Seychelles, ■ Ind. Ocean ...3 E12
Sfax, Tunisia ...27 B7
Shache, China ...22 C2
Shanghai, China ...22 C7
Shannon, ≈ Ire. ...11 D2
Shantou, China ...22 D6
Shapinsay, U.K. ...10 B6
Sheffield, U.K. ...8 D6
Shenyang, China ...22 B7
Sherwood Forest, U.K. ...8 D6
Shetland, □ U.K. ...10 A7
Shikoku, □ Japan ...21 C3
Shimonoseki, Japan ...21 C2
Shiráz, Iran ...25 C4
Shizuoka, Japan ...21 B6
Sholapur, India ...24 E4
Shreveport, U.S.A. ...37 D8
Shrewsbury, U.K. ...8 E5
Shropshire, □ U.K. ...9 E5
Siam = Thailand, ■ Asia ...23 B2
Sibiu, Rom. ...17 F12
Sichuan, □ China ...22 D5
Sicilia, □ Italy ...14 F5
Siena, Italy ...14 C4
Sierra Leone, ■ Africa ...26 G2
Sierra Nevada, U.S.A. ...36 C3
Silver City, Panama ...38 H14
Simpson Desert, Australia ...32 C6
Singapore, ■ Asia ...23 C2
Sioux City, U.S.A. ...37 B7
Sioux Falls, U.S.A. ...37 B7
Siracusa, Italy ...14 F6
Sitges, Spain ...13 B6
Sjælland, Den. ...7 J11
Skagerrak, Europe ...7 H10
Skien, Norw. ...7 G10
Skikda, Algeria ...26 A6
Skopje, Macedonia ...15 C9
Skye, I. of, U.K. ...10 D2
Slieve Aughty, Ire. ...11 C3
Slieve Bloom, Ire. ...11 C4
Slieve Mish, Ire. ...11 D2
Sligo, Ire. ...11 B3
Slough, U.K. ...9 F7
Slovak Rep., ■ Europe ...17 D9
Slovenia, ■ Europe ...16 B6
Snake, ≈ U.S.A. ...36 A3
Snowdon, U.K. ...8 D3
Society Is., Pac. Ocean ...2 F2
Socotra, Yemen ...25 D4
Söderhamn, Swed. ...7 F14
Sofiya, Bulg. ...15 C10
Sogn og Fjordane, □ Norw. ...7 F9
Solimoes, ≈ Brazil ...40 D5
Solomon Is., ■ Pac. Ocean ...3 F17
Solway Firth, U.K. ...8 C4
Somali Rep., ■ Africa ...30 E8
Somerset, □ U.K. ...9 F4
Somerset I., Canada ...34 A10
Sør-Trondelag, □ Norw. ...6 D12
Soria, Spain ...13 B4
Sorocaba, Brazil ...42 A7
Sosnowiec, Poland ...17 C9
Sŏul, S. Korea ...22 C7
Sousse, Tunisia ...27 A7
South Africa, ■ Africa ...29 L3
South Australia, □ Australia ...32 D5
South Bend, U.S.A. ...37 B9
South Carolina, □ U.S.A. ...37 D10
South China Sea, Asia ...23 B3
South Dakota, □ U.S.A. ...36 B6
South Downs, U.K. ...9 G7
South Georgia, Atl. Ocean ...42 G9
South Glamorgan, □ U.K. ...9 F4
South Island, N.Z. ...31 K3
South Korea, ■ Asia ...22 C7
South Ronaldsay, U.K. ...10 C6
South Shields, U.K. ...8 C6
South Uist, U.K. ...10 D1
South Yorkshire, □ U.K. ...8 D6
Southampton, U.K. ...9 G6
Southampton I., Canada ...35 B11
Southend, U.K. ...9 F8
Southern Alps, N.Z. ...31 K3
Southern Ocean, ...3 G12
Southern Uplands, U.K. ...10 F5
Southport, U.K. ...8 D4
Soutpansberge, S. Africa ...29 J5
Spain, ■ Europe ...13 B4
Spandau, Ger. ...16 B6
Spanish Town, Jamaica ...38 K17
Spencer Gulf, Australia ...32 E6
Sperrin Mts., U.K. ...11 B4
Spessart, Ger. ...16 D4
Split, Croatia ...14 C7
Spokane, U.S.A. ...36 A3
Sporádhes Voríai, Greece ...15 E11
Springfield, U.S.A. ...37 B12
Springs, S. Africa ...29 K5
Sri Lanka, ■ Asia ...24 G5
Srinagar, India ...24 B3

Index

St. Albans, *U.K.* 9 F7
St. Andrews, *U.K.* 10 E6
St. Austell, *U.K.* 9 G3
St. Boniface, *Canada* 34 D10
St. Christopher-Nevis = St. Kitts -
  Nevis, ■ *W. Indies* 38 K19
St. Croix, *W. Indies* 39 D12
St. - Étienne, *France* 12 D6
St. - Gallen, *Switz.* 16 E4
St. George's, *Grenada* 38 Q20
St. George's Channel, *Europe* 11 E5
St. Helena, *Atl. Ocean* 30 G3
St. Helens, *U.K.* 8 D5
St. John's, *Antigua* 38 K20
St. John's, *Canada* 35 D14
St. Kitts - Nevis, ■ *W. Indies* 38 K19
St. Lawrence, ≈ *Canada* 35 D14
St. Louis, *U.S.A.* 37 C8
St. Lucia, ■ *W. Indies* 38 P21
St. Maarten, □ *W. Indies* 38 J18
St. Malo, *France* 12 B2
St. Martin, □ *W. Indies* 38 J18
St. Michael's Mt., *U.K.* 9 G2
St. Nazaire, *France* 12 C2
St. Paul, *U.S.A.* 37 B8
St. Peterburg, *Russia* 18 D4
St. Petersburg, *U.S.A.* 37 E10
St. Pierre et Miquelon, □ *N. Amer.* ..35 D14
St. Thomas, *W. Indies* 39 D12
St. - Denis, *France* 12 B5
St. - Tropez, *France* 12 E7
St. Vincent & the Grenadines,
  ■ *W. Indies* 38 P20
Stafford, *U.K.* 8 E5
Staffordshire, □ *U.K.* 8 E5
Staines, *U.K.* 9 F7
Stalingrad = Volgograd, *Russia* 18 E5
Stanley, *Falkland Is.* 42 G5
Stara Planina, *Bulg.* 15 C11
Stavanger, *Norw.* 7 G8
Steiermark, □ *Austria* 16 E7
Sterea Ellas, □ *Greece* 15 E9
Stewart I., *N.Z.* 31 M1
Stirling, *U.K.* 10 E5
Stockholm, *Swed.* 7 G15
Stockport, *U.K.* 8 D5
Stockton, *U.K.* 8 C6
Stockton, *U.S.A.* 36 C2
Stoke-on-Trent, *U.K.* 8 D5
Stonehenge, *U.K.* 9 F6
Stourbridge, *U.K.* 9 E5
Strabane, *U.K.* 11 B4
Stralsund, *Ger.* 16 A6
Strasbourg, *France* 12 B7
Stratford-on-Avon, *U.K.* 9 E6
Strath Spey, *U.K.* 10 D5
Strathclyde, □ *U.K.* 10 F3
Stromeferry, *U.K.* 10 D3
Stronsay, *U.K.* 10 B6
Stuttgart, *Ger.* 16 D4
Subotica, *Yug.* 15 A8
Sucre, *Bolivia* 40 G5
Sudan, ■ *Africa* 27 E10
Sudbury, *Canada* 35 D11
Suez Canal, *Egypt* 25 B2
Suez = El Suweis, *Egypt* 27 C11
Suffolk, □ *U.K.* 9 E8
Sulawesi, *Indonesia* 23 D4
Sumatera, *Indonesia* 23 D2
Sumba, *Indonesia* 23 D4
Sumbawa, *Indonesia* 23 D3
Sunderland, *U.K.* 8 C6
Sundsvall, *Swed.* 6 E14
Superior, L., *N. Amer.* 37 A9
Surabaja, *Indonesia* 23 D3
Surat, *India* 24 D3
Surinam, ■ *S. Amer.* 41 C7
Surrey, □ *U.K.* 9 F7
Sutton-in-Ashfield, *U.K.* 8 D6
Suva, *Fiji* 31 D8
Suzhou, *China* 22 C7
Svendborg, *Den.* 7 J11
Sverdlovsk = Yekaterinburg, *Russia* 18 D7
Swansea, *U.K.* 9 F4
Swaziland, ■ *Africa* 29 K6
Sweden, ■ *Europe* 7 F13
Swindon, *U.K.* 9 F6
Switzerland, ■ *Europe* 16 E3
Sydney, *Australia* 33 E9
Syracuse, *U.S.A.* 37 B11
Syria, ■ *Asia* 25 B2
Syrian Desert, *Asia* 25 B2
Szczecin, *Poland* 16 B7
Szeged, *Hungary* 17 E10

T

Tabrīz, *Iran* 25 B3
Tacoma, *U.S.A.* 36 A2
Taegu, *S. Korea* 22 C7
Tahiti, *Pac. Ocean* 2 E2
Taibei, *Taiwan* 22 D7
Tainan, *Taiwan* 22 D7
Taiwan, ■ *Asia* 22 D7
Taiyuan, *China* 22 C6
Taizhong, *Taiwan* 22 D7
Tajikistan, ■ *Asia* 18 F7
Takamatsu, *Japan* 21 B4
Talcahuano, *Chile* 42 D2

Tallinn, *Estonia* 18 D3
Tamil Nadu, □ *India* 24 F4
Tampa, *U.S.A.* 37 E10
Tampere, *Fin.* 7 F17
Tampico, *Mexico* 38 C5
Tamworth, *U.K.* 9 E6
Tane-ga-Shima, *Japan* 21 D2
Tanga, *Tanzania* 28 F7
Tanganyika, L., *Africa* 28 F5
Tangier, *Morocco* 26 A3
Tangshan, *China* 22 C6
Tanimbar Is., *Indonesia* 23 D5
Tanta, *Egypt* 27 B11
Tanzania, ■ *Africa* 28 F7
Tarābulus, *Lebanon* 25 B2
Tarābulus, *Libya* 27 B7
Taranto, *Italy* 14 D7
Tarragona, *Spain* 13 B6
Tarrasa, *Spain* 13 B6
Tashkent, *Uzbekistan* 18 E7
Tasman Sea, *Pac. Ocean* 31 J2
Tasmania, *Australia* 33 G8
Tauern, *Austria* 16 E6
Taunton, *U.K.* 9 F4
Taunus, *Ger.* 16 C4
Tay, ≈ *U.K.* 10 E5
Tayside, □ *U.K.* 10 E5
Tbilisi, *Georgia* 18 E5
Tchad, L., *Chad* 27 F7
Teesside, *U.K.* 8 C6
Tegucigalpa, *Honduras* 38 E7
Tehrān, *Iran* 25 B4
Tehuantepec, Istme de, *Mexico* ..38 D5
Tejo, ≈ *Port.* 13 C1
Tel Aviv - Yafo, *Israel* 25 B2
Telemark, □ *Norw.* 7 G10
Telford, *U.K.* 8 E5
Tenerife, *Canary Is.* 26 C1
Tennessee, □ *U.S.A.* 37 C9
Tennessee, ≈ *U.S.A.* 37 C9
Teresina, *Brazil* 41 E10
Terni, *Italy* 14 C5
Teruel, *Spain* 13 B5
Tetouan, *Morocco* 26 A3
Teutoburger Wald, *Ger.* 16 B4
Tevere, ≈ *Italy* 14 C5
Texas, □ *U.S.A.* 36 D6
Thailand, ■ *Asia* 23 B2
Thames, ≈ *U.K.* 9 F8
Thásos, *Greece* 15 D11
The Hague = 's-Gravenhage, *Neth.* .16 B2
Thessalia, □ *Greece* 15 E10
Thessaloníka, *Greece* 15 D10
Thies, *Senegal* 26 F1
Thráki, □ *Greece* 15 D11
Thunder Bay, *Canada* 35 D11
Thüringer Wald, *Ger.* 16 C5
Thurles, *Ire.* 11 D4
Thurso, *U.K.* 10 C5
Tianjin, *China* 22 C6
Tiber = Tevere, ≈ *Italy* 14 C5
Tibesti, *Chad* 27 D8
Tibet = Xizang, □ *China* 22 C3
Tientsin = Tianjin, *China* 22 C6
Tierra del Fuego, *S. Amer.* 42 G3
Tigris, ≈ *Iraq* 25 B3
Tijuana, *Mexico* 38 A1
Tilburg, *Neth.* 16 C2
Timaru, *N.Z.* 31 L3
Timişoara, *Rom.* 17 F10
Timor, *Indonesia* 23 D4
Tínos, *Greece* 15 F11
Tipperary, □ *Ire.* 11 D4
Tipperary, *Ire.* 11 D3
Tipton, *U.K.* 9 E5
Tirana, *Alb.* 15 D8
Tiree, *U.K.* 10 E2
Tirol, □ *Austria* 16 E5
Tiruchchirappalli, *India* 24 F4
Titicaca, L., *S. Amer.* 40 G5
Titograd = Podgorica, *Yug.* 15 C8
Tizi-Ouzou, *Algeria* 26 A5
Tobago, *W. Indies* 39 E12
Togo, ■ *Africa* 26 G5
Tokelau Is., *Pac. Ocean* 2 E1
Tōkyo, *Japan* 21 B6
Toledo, *Spain* 13 C3
Toledo, *U.S.A.* 37 B10
Toluca, *Mexico* 38 D5
Tomsk, *Russia* 18 D9
Tonga, ■ *Pac. Ocean* 31 D11
Toowoomba, *Australia* 33 D9
Topeka, *U.S.A.* 37 C7
Torbay, *U.K.* 9 G4
Torino, *Italy* 14 B2
Toronto, *Canada* 35 D12
Torquay, *U.K.* 9 G4
Torremolinos, *Spain* 13 D3
Torrens, L., *Australia* 33 E6
Torreón, *Mexico* 38 B4
Tortosa, *Spain* 13 B6
Toruń, *Poland* 17 B9
Toscana, □ *Italy* 14 C4
Toulon, *France* 12 E6
Toulouse, *France* 12 E4
Touraine, □ *France* 12 C4
Tourcoing, *Belgium* 16 C1
Tours, *France* 12 C4
Townsville, *Australia* 33 B8

Toyama, *Japan* 21 A5
Toyohashi, *Japan* 21 B5
Toyonaka, *Japan* 21 B4
Tralee, *Ire.* 11 D2
Transilvania, *Rom.* 17 E12
Trápani, *Italy* 14 E5
Trelleborg, *Swed.* 7 J12
Trentino Alto-Adige, □ *Italy* 14 A4
Treviso, *Italy* 14 B5
Trier, *Ger.* 16 D3
Trieste, *Italy* 14 B5
Trincomalee, *Sri Lanka* 24 G5
Trinidad & Tobago, ■ *W. Indies* ..39 E12
Tripoli = Tarābulus, *Libya* 27 B7
Tristan da Cunha, *Atl. Ocean* 2 F9
Trois-Rivières, *Canada* 35 D12
Trollhättan, *Swed.* 7 G12
Troms, □ *Norw.* 6 B15
Tromso, *Norw.* 6 B15
Trondheim, *Norw.* 6 E11
Trossachs, *U.K.* 10 E4
Trujillo, *Peru* 40 E3
Tsugaru-Kaikyŏ, *Japan* 21 F11
Tsushima, *Japan* 21 H8
Tuamotu Arch., *Pac. Ocean* 2 E3
Tubuai Is., *Pac. Ocean* 2 F2
Tucson, *U.S.A.* 36 D4
Tula, *Russia* 18 D4
Tullamore, *Ire.* 11 C4
Tulsa, *U.S.A.* 37 C7
Tulua, *Colombia* 40 C3
Tunis, *Tunisia* 26 A6
Tunisia, ■ *Africa* 26 A6
Turin = Torino, *Italy* 14 B2
Turkana, L., *Kenya* 28 D7
Turkey, ■ *Asia* 25 B2
Turkmenistan, ■ *Asia* 18 F6
Turku, *Fin.* 7 F17
Turnu-Severin, *Rom.* 17 F11
Turun ja Pori, □ *Fin.* 7 F17
Tuvalu, ■ *Pac. Ocean* 3 E18
Tver, *Russia* 18 D4
Tyler, *U.S.A.* 37 D7
Tyne & Wear, □ *U.K.* 8 C6
Tynemouth, *U.K.* 8 C6
Tyrrhenian Sea, *Italy* 14 E5

U

Uberaba, *Brazil* 41 G9
Uddevalla, *Swed.* 7 G11
Udine, *Italy* 14 A5
Ufa, *Russia* 18 D6
Uganda, ■ *Africa* 28 D6
Ujpest, *Hungary* 17 E9
Ujung Pandang, *Indonesia* 23 D3
Ukraine, ■ *Europe* 18 E4
Ulaanbaatar, *Mong.* 22 B5
Ulan Ude, *Russia* 19 D11
Ullapool, *U.K.* 10 D3
Ulm, *Ger.* 16 D4
Ulster, □ *U.K.* 11 B4
Umbria, □ *Italy* 14 C5
Ungava Pen., *Canada* 35 C12
United Arab Emirates, ■ *Asia* ..25 C4
United Kingdom, ■ *Europe* 4 E5
United States of America, ■
  N. Amer. 36 C6
Unst, *U.K.* 10 A8
Uppsala, *Swed.* 7 G14
Urmia, L., *Iran* 25 B3
Uruguay, ■ *S. Amer.* 42 C5
Uruguay, ≈ *S. Amer.* 42 C5
Urumqi, *China* 22 B3
Usti nad Labem, *Czech Rep.* 16 C7
Utah, □ *U.S.A.* 36 C4
Utrecht, *Neth.* 16 B2
Uttar Pradesh, □ *India* 24 C5
Uudenmaa, □ *Fin.* 7 F18
Uzbekistan, ■ *Asia* 18 E7

V

Vaal, ≈ *S. Africa* 29 K4
Vaasa, □ *Fin.* 6 E17
Vadso, *Norw.* 6 A20
Valence, *France* 12 D6
Valencia, □ *Spain* 13 C5
Valencia, *Spain* 13 C5
Valencia, *Venezuela* 40 A5
Valladolid, *Spain* 13 B3
Valle d'Aosta, *Italy* 14 B2
Valletta, *Malta* 14 G6
Valparaíso, *Chile* 42 C2
Vancouver, *Canada* 34 D7
Vancouver I., *Canada* 34 D7
Vanuatu, ■ *Pac. Ocean* 3 E18
Varanasi, *India* 24 C5
Värmland, □ *Swed.* 7 G12
Varna, *Bulg.* 15 C12
Västerås, *Swed.* 7 G14
Vasterbotten, □ *Norw.* 6 D14
Vasternorrland, □ *Norw.* 6 E14
Västervik, *Swed.* 7 H14
Västmanland, □ *Swed.* 7 G14
Vatnajökull, *Iceland* 6 D5
Veneto, □ *Italy* 14 B4
Venézia, *Italy* 14 B5

Venezuela, ■ *S. Amer.* 40 B5
Veracruz, *Mexico* 38 D5
Vereeniging, *S. Africa* 29 K5
Vermont, □ *U.S.A.* 37 B12
Verona, *Italy* 14 B4
Versailles, *France* 12 B5
Vest-Agder, □ *Norw.* 7 G9
Vesterålen, *Norw.* 6 B13
Vestfjorden, *Norw.* 6 B13
Vesuvio, *Italy* 14 D6
Viborg, *Den.* 7 H10
Vichy, *France* 12 C5
Victoria, *Australia* 33 F7
Victoria, *Canada* 34 D7
Victoria Falls, *Zimbabwe* 29 H5
Victoria I., *Canada* 34 A8
Victoria, L., *Africa* 28 E6
Vienna = Wien, *Austria* 16 D8
Vientos, Paso de los, *W. Indies* 39 C10
Vietnam, ■ *Asia* 23 B2
Vigo, *Spain* 13 A1
Vilnius, *Lithuania* 18 D3
Viña del Mar, *Chile* 42 C2
Viña I., *W. Indies* 39 D12
Virginia, □ *U.S.A.* 37 C11
Visby, *Swed.* 7 H15
Vitória, *Brazil* 41 H10
Vitoria, *Spain* 13 A4
Vladivostok, *Russia* 19 E14
Vojvodina, □ *Yug.* 15 B8
Volga, ≈ *Russia* 18 E5
Volgograd, *Russia* 18 E5
Vólos, *Greece* 15 E10
Volta, L., *Ghana* 26 G4
Voralberg, □ *Austria* 16 E4
Voronezh, *Russia* 18 D4
Vyatka, *Russia* 18 D5

W

Waco, *U.S.A.* 37 D7
Wâd Medanî, *Sudan* 27 F11
Wakayama, *Japan* 21 B4
Wakefield, *U.K.* 8 D6
Wakkanai, *Japan* 21 E11
Wałbrzych, *Poland* 16 C8
Wales, □ *U.K.* 9 E4
Wallasey, *U.K.* 8 D4
Wallsend, *U.K.* 8 B6
Walney I., *U.K.* 8 C4
Walsall, *U.K.* 9 E5
Walvisbaai, *Namibia* 29 J2
Wanganui, *N.Z.* 31 H5
Warley, *U.K.* 9 E5
Warrington, *U.K.* 8 D5
Warszawa, *Poland* 17 B10
Warwick, *U.K.* 9 E6
Warwickshire, □ *U.K.* 9 E6
Wash, The, ≈ *U.K.* 8 E8
Washington, □ *U.S.A.* 36 A2
Washington D.C., *U.S.A.* 37 C11
Waterbury, *U.S.A.* 37 B12
Waterford, *Ire.* 11 D4
Watford, *U.K.* 9 F7
Weald, The, *U.K.* 9 F7
Welkom, *S. Africa* 29 K5
Wellesley Is., *Australia* 33 B6
Wellington, *N.Z.* 31 J5
Wellington I., *Chile* 42 F2
Wenzhou, *China* 22 D7
West Bromwich, *U.K.* 9 E5
West Glamorgan, □ *U.K.* 9 F4
West Indies 39 D10
West Midlands, □ *U.K.* 9 E6
West Sussex, □ *U.K.* 9 G7
West Virginia, □ *U.S.A.* 37 C10
West Yorkshire, □ *U.K.* 8 D6
Western Australia, □ *Oceania* 32 C3
Western Is., □ *U.K.* 10 D1
Western Sahara, ■ *Africa* 26 C2
Western Samoa, ■ *Pac. Ocean* 2 E1
Westerwald, *Ger.* 16 C3
Westmeath, □ *Ire.* 11 C4
Weston-super-Mare, *U.K.* 9 F5
Westray, *U.K.* 10 B5
Wexford, *Ire.* 11 D5
Weymouth, *U.K.* 9 G5
Whalsay, *U.K.* 10 A8
White Nile = Nîl el Abyad, ≈ *Africa* ..27 E11
White Sea = Beloye More, *Russia* ...18 C4
Whitehaven, *U.K.* 8 C4
Whitehorse, *Canada* 34 B6
Wichita, *U.S.A.* 37 C7
Wichita Falls, *U.S.A.* 36 D7
Wick, *U.K.* 10 C5
Wicklow, *Ire.* 11 D5
Wien, *Austria* 16 D8
Wiesbaden, *Ger.* 16 C4
Wigan, *U.K.* 8 D5
Wight, I. of, □ *U.K.* 9 G6
Wilhelmshaven, *Ger.* 16 B4
Wilmington, *U.S.A.* 37 C11
Wiltshire, □ *U.K.* 9 F6
Winchester, *U.K.* 9 F6
Windermere, L., *U.K.* 8 C5
Windhoek, *Namibia* 29 J3
Windsor, *U.K.* 9 F7
Windsor, *Canada* 35 D11
Windward Is., *W. Indies* 39 E12

Winnipeg, *Canada* 34 D10
Winnipeg, L., *Canada* 34 C10
Winston Salem, *U.S.A.* 37 C10
Winterthur, *Switz.* 16 E4
Wirral, The, *U.K.* 8 D4
Wisconsin, □ *U.S.A.* 37 B9
Wishaw, *U.K.* 10 F5
Włocławek, *Poland* 17 B9
Woking, *U.K.* 9 F7
Wollongong, *Australia* 33 E9
Wolverhampton, *U.K.* 9 E5
Worcester, *U.K.* 9 E5
Worcester, *U.S.A.* 37 B12
Workington, *U.K.* 8 C4
Worksop, *U.K.* 8 D6
Worms, *Ger.* 16 D4
Worthing, *U.K.* 9 G7
Wrexham, *U.K.* 8 D4
Wrocław, *Poland* 16 C8
Wuhan, *China* 22 C6
Wuhu, *China* 22 C6
Wuppertal, *Ger.* 16 C3
Würzburg, *Ger.* 16 D4
Wyoming, □ *U.S.A.* 36 B5

X

Xi'an, *China* 22 C5
Xiaguan, *China* 22 D5
Xingu, ≈ *Brazil* 41 D8
Xinjiang Uygur, □ *China* 22 B3
Xizang, □ *China* 22 C3
Xuzhou, *China* 22 C6

Y

Yakushima, *Japan* 21 D2
Yakutsk, *Russia* 19 C13
Yamagata, *Japan* 21 G11
Yaoundé, *Cameroon* 28 D2
Yaroslavl, *Russia* 18 D4
Yazd, *Iran* 25 B4
Yell, *U.K.* 10 A7
Yellow Sea, *Asia* 22 C7
Yellowknife, *Canada* 34 B8
Yellowstone National Park, *U.S.A.* ..36 B4
Yemen, ■ *Asia* 25 D4
Yenisey, ≈ *Russia* 18 C9
Yeovil, *U.K.* 9 G5
Yerevan, *Armenia* 18 E5
Yining, *China* 22 B3
Yokohama, *Japan* 21 B6
Yokosuka, *Japan* 21 B6
York, *U.K.* 8 D6
Youghal, *Ire.* 11 E4
Ystad, *Swed.* 7 J12
Yucatan, □ *Mexico* 38 D7
Yugoslavia, ■ *Europe* 15 B9
Yukon, ≈ *N. Amer.* 34 B4
Yukon Territory, □ *Canada* 34 B6

Z

Zabrze, *Poland* 17 C9
Zagazig, *Egypt* 27 B11
Zagreb, *Croatia* 14 B6
Zagros Mts., *Iran* 25 B3
Zaïre, ≈ *Africa* 28 D4
Zaïre, ■ *Africa* 28 E4
Zákinthos, *Greece* 15 F9
Zambezi, ≈ *Africa* 29 H6
Zambia, ■ *Africa* 29 G5
Zamora, *Spain* 13 B3
Zanzibar, *Tanzania* 28 F7
Zaporozhye, *Ukraine* 18 E4
Zaragoza, *Spain* 13 B5
Zaria, *Nigeria* 26 F6
Zemlya Frantsa Iosifa, *Russia* 18 B6
Zhanghua, *Taiwan* 22 D7
Zhangjiakou, *China* 22 B6
Zhengzhou, *China* 22 C6
Zhenjiang, *China* 22 C6
Zibo, *China* 22 C6
Zigong, *China* 22 D5
Zimbabwe, ■ *Africa* 29 H5
Zürich, *Switz.* 16 E4
Zwickau, *Ger.* 16 C6